A MANOR THROUGH
FOUR CENTURIES

OXFORD UNIVERSITY PRESS
AMEN HOUSE, E.C. 4
London Edinburgh Glasgow New York
Toronto Melbourne Capetown Bombay
Calcutta Madras
HUMPHREY MILFORD
PUBLISHER TO THE UNIVERSITY

ONE OF TWO GARDEN TOWERS ON THE TERRACE AT ROYDON
Tudor period, *c.* 1530 (Chimneys restored)

A MANOR THROUGH FOUR CENTURIES

BY

A. R. COOK

OXFORD UNIVERSITY PRESS
LONDON NEW YORK TORONTO
1938

PRINTED IN GREAT BRITAIN

TO MY FATHER

IN GRATEFUL TRIBUTE TO HIS
UNVARYING EFFORTS TO MAINTAIN ROYDON
AND THE TRADITIONS OF ITS OWNERS
THROUGH THESE CHANGING
TIMES

INTRODUCTION

MUCH has already been written of Kent; no English county can claim a fuller measure of historical interest, nor the service of abler county historians. Kent has played a leading part in shaping the destinies of our country. The opinions and tenets of its people through the centuries have provided a reliable indication of the temper of England as a whole. Yet there is much that still remains to be collected and brought to light from private documents and diaries, and there is much also to be gleaned from parish records and local museums, whose evidence takes us back a long way into the past.

It is not a simple matter to make a consecutive story out of such materials; I have endeavoured, probably with indifferent success, to put together something with a thread running through it—the story of a manor-house in which several families in succession have resided continuously for over four hundred years.

I do not pretend to have given more than a glimpse of manorial history and customs, nor to have accounted for more than a fragment of the changes affecting the country squire over this length of time. Nor have I attempted to fulfil the task of writing a history of any one of the several families that fall within the purlieu of this book. Roydon is chosen because it is a fair example of an old English country house, modest in size and set in typical surroundings; and, perhaps more particularly, because it happens to be the author's own home; he therefore may lay some claim to an intimate knowledge of it.

Fortunately the place can boast a fair share of adventure during the various periods of its existence, considering that it does not aspire to fame through connexion with any great personages or events. It may for that reason appeal to the larger number of folk.

If I have at times wandered rather far afield from Kent,

or trespassed upon the well-trodden paths of history pure and simple, it has been mainly in order to notice and compare incidents that have occurred in other parts of England of a similar nature to the adventures of our own county and the manor, or to trace the further activities of the families concerned and their relations elsewhere.

It has also been my endeavour to show in a wider sense the bearing that certain events in the past have had, directly or indirectly, upon the subject, in order that we may the more clearly read the signs of the times and more jealously guard the present and the future of our own countryside.

In East Peckham Church I have perused many memorials, whose evidence I acknowledge for many of the records of Hextals, Whetenhalls, Roydons, and Twysdens. To its vicar, the Reverend F. W. Bennitt, I am indebted for many of the contemporary facts gleaned from the Parish Registers, and not less to its late vicar, Canon Ryley, for the many delightful anecdotes he collected for publication in the parish magazines during the twenty-odd years that he was vicar of East Peckham.

To the late Sir John Twisden of Bradbourne, the authority on all Twysden muniments and family records, I owe a debt of gratitude for being kindness itself in inviting me to Bradbourne to inspect his collection of notes. To Mr. E. B. Royden also, who some years ago published a delightful book, *Three Roydon Families*,[1] I must acknowledge my thanks for putting at my disposal certain plates for reproduction in this book, together with much information freely offered concerning the early history of the Reydons of Suffolk, the ancestors of the Roydons of Kent. I must also pay a tribute to those eminent contemporary historians from whose works I have quoted: Sir G. M. Trevelyan (*History of England*) and Sir Charles Petrie (*The Four Georges*), and, last but not least, to the Kent Archaeological Society for allowing me to extract from their earlier volumes the extensive quotations I have made from the 'Journal of Sir Roger Twysden'.

[1] T. & T. Clark, Ltd., Edinburgh, 1924.

Finally, I would mention the problem of maintaining the fabric of East Peckham Church in a good state of preservation. The parish is sparsely populated for its size, and the Church treasury, like that of all old churches, has too many calls upon it to make possible the setting aside of an adequate fund for conserving the building itself. Moreover, when money for the fabric of a medieval church is required, it is usually needed urgently and in substantial measure, in all probability to avert some pressing disaster from overtaking it.

With those who have the welfare of St. Michael's at heart, I feel that a suitable object for the proceeds of this book would be to inaugurate a fund devoted expressly to preserving its fabric against those mischances that from time to time occur and threaten to undermine the stability of our ancient buildings.

A. R. C.

PETTERIDGE PLACE,
  BRENCHLEY, KENT

May 1938

CONTENTS

LIST OF ILLUSTRATIONS

CHAPTER I

THE PROTECTION OF OUR HERITAGE

'The greatest advantages men have by riches are to give, to build, to plant and make pleasant scenes . . .' Sir William Temple.

THE main object of this book is to stimulate interest in the problem of the country in relation to the town; to examine its future in the midst of a social advancement that has moved at an unprecedented rate in the last fifteen years—and still continues to do so—and to reconcile its needs with the atmosphere of the past, an atmosphere which invariably reminds us of the best things we have done and the greatest heights we have achieved. A stage has been reached—though the situation is never for a moment static—where a breathing-space is necessary if we are to harness a pre-selected order of things to the human urge to move outwards and upwards. The strongest forces, whether progressive, reactionary, self-interested, or self-protective, must be mobilized in order that the torrent may be directed into the moderate valleys rather than allowed to rush headlong over the most precipitous falls.

Let us examine the steps which have led to the present incidence of the country-side. The subject of a landscape painting by Constable, however much the picture may have been inspired by a divine creation, did not just happen to fall there by chance. It was brought about by centuries of development based upon historical factors vitally connected with the inhabitants' ability to exist there through years of changing circumstances and conditions. For long periods there was no change; at other times comparatively short spells of intense national stress wrought fundamental changes. Yet until the last hundred years these changes could always be traced to some definite cause, and the consequent movement in landscape or population was so gradual as to be scarcely perceptible. The social historian who bravely attempts to analyse the evolution of the last half-century into a series of well-defined movements with their attributive causes will be taking on an unenviable task. The Great War, the motor-car, and the wireless will probably be the salient points of successive bounds by which he will endeavour to proceed. He will probably lay stress upon the lengthening of human life and the great benefit which shorter hours of work have conferred upon mankind. But they will not be of great benefit unless the extra leisure derived from them is planned with forethought and actuated by the desire to spend it advantageously. To pass the time in search of new amusements is to waste a valuable asset which has been hardly gained by man in his advancing civilization, and which is therefore worthy of being put to the best possible use. Leisure must be recognized as a remission of tax upon working effort and the proceeds turned to good account.

The unifying effects of mass-production upon individual purpose may be the inevitable outcome of a highly organized social system, and may indeed be apparent in a high standard of living; but such benefits, if they may claim to be so, must be made to give adequate compensation for the moral destruction brought about by the machine, lest the machine itself, like Moloch, devour men's souls, giving only in return a constant desire for motion and its accompanying emotion.

Nature is forcing upon us a powerful reaction the result of which cannot yet be fully measured—a revolution caused by increasing contact with the machine in everyday life and the speed-up in living. But a change is assuredly taking place and the vicious circle is being broken. There is already a tendency for the pace to slow down—at least during the leisure hours—already a desire to get away from the crowd and live in the peace and stillness of the country as opposed to working in the din and bustle of the town. A worthy object of any newly gained leisure might be some appreciation of the country wherein we move, of its beauty and the refinement lying in the ancient monuments which are an essential part of its history. The soil is our heritage and the country our solace; but no village is any longer immune, no lane is left unexplored. The ever-increasing use of the roads is evidence enough of the part taken by the motor-car in the social revolution. The heart of rural England has been plumbed to its depths. Millions who until recently have never seen open fields and woods have begun to experience the thrill of awakening to a sense of beauty, to the growing benefit of mankind.

What are the main causes of the encroachment of the urban population upon the country that has been so accelerated in recent years, and of the formation of successive circles round the larger towns, like ripples on a pond emanating from a stone thrown into it? Let us enumerate the facts that in our view have set in motion the amazing and rapid movement that is beginning to possess the country-side.

1. The high standard of living, brought about largely by social expenditure and by the normal incentive to climb higher up the social scale.
2. The vast improvement in transport services and the cheapening of fares.
3. The crowding of population into the cities and the consequent urgency of the problems of housing and slum clearance.
4. The opportunities of the land-speculator and the building-speculator of profiting by the necessity for providing any type of accommodation to help satisfy this need.
5. The pressure put upon successive governments by the competition among their parties as to which could most rapidly produce the greatest number of houses, regardless of order.
6. The preponderance of the mass-minded, who are sensible only of what is put immediately in front of them.

7. The apathy of most owners of extensive property, and their reluctance towards organizing themselves for their own protection until it is too late.

The vast majority of this country's population is urban by environment—that is to say, born and bred in the town. The rest are mostly urban-minded. The girl in the town must always be telling her cousin in the country stories of the wages to be earned, the shows to be seen, the friends to be had in town. The village girl's first reaction is to jump into a bus and try it out for herself.

The men have been driven into the cities by the lure of employment and equally forcibly by the lack of it. From this point it is not difficult to arrive at the stage where the housing problem started to become acute. Interrupted by the War, social legislation was demanded in turn by socialists themselves and those who, in opposition, were determined not to be outdone but rather to steal the enemies' thunder. Any one who came forward with a housing scheme of sufficient magnitude was hailed with open arms as a public benefactor and immediately let loose.

The lure of profit—and much profit—galvanized the building-speculator into activity. Building societies were too busy snapping up opportunities which the financial rewards offered to think of trying to educate their clients in developing the aesthetic side of their homes. The motley grew apace and spoliation with it. The Town and Country Planning Acts and the Ribbon Development Act came, not in their proper course before, but, by way of protest, after the evil had begun—a natural expression of resentment at the indescribable chaos which was being born. The planning of our towns and villages, with due respect to the beauties of nature, will become a matter of real interest and importance to the community as soon as ever appreciation of them begins to make itself felt. A growing restraint is already being shown by the road-user, whether in motor-car, on bicycle, or on foot; motorists in their recently annexed triumphs over time and distance are unconsciously assuming a respect for things growing and their ownership, the first signs of a veneration for, and understanding of, the country and its remoteness.

Professor Trevelyan, commenting on the growing despoliation of rural England in *Britain and the Beast*,[1] says:

'In old days the refusal of the State to concern itself with questions of amenity was natural, because the ordinary development of the country did little harm to beauty; and the citadels of rural beauty—parks, woods, country houses—scattered thickly over the land, were kept up by individual owners. Now the development of motor traction turns every "beauty spot" into an "eligible building site" and the State by its taxation forces owners to sell, while at the same time it refuses to control the evil consequences of the sale of private property which its financial policy compels. The State is Socialist enough to destroy by taxation the classes that used to preserve rural amenity; but it is still too Conservative to interfere in the purposes to which land is put by speculators to whom the land is sold.'

The argument for standing in the way of progress is untenable because progress is a matter of fact. It has behind it the inevitability of the law of expansion; an outlet must be found or the container will burst. The essential thing is to plan that expansion and control it, for it is the lack of such control in planning that we have been suffering from. The truth of this is being recognized with belated regret to-day, resulting in an attempt, if not to cry halt, at least to gain a breathing-space and see where mistakes have already been irretrievably committed and where they may be avoided if only we will get to the root of the problem and grapple with the facts. To rally the forces capable of appreciating where England's beauty lies and of knowing how to develop utility combined with beauty is of the first importance. That utility is an adjunct to beauty in this modern age cannot be denied; but it must be rightly planned.

As in all good planning, whether for industry or for

[1] J. M. Dent & Sons, Ltd.

social welfare, it is impossible to correlate these forces unless government, both local and central, intervenes and gives its aid in order that private enterprise may be set upon the right path. The merits of co-operation with the various bodies already in existence for the preservation of amenities, such as The Central Landowners Association, The Forestry Commission, and the embryo Association of Country House Owners, cannot be too highly stressed. These bodies have already formed the rallying-ground of individuals who have the beauty of the country at heart and possess the desire to see that good planning is achieved. They are the nucleus around which the best schemes will be evolved and the channels through which they can best be supported and carried out.

Many benefactors, for instance the late Lord Curzon and the late Lord Conway, have made it their hobby to uncover and restore architectural beauties of the past which have been allowed to fall into decay. Others have set themselves the equally fascinating task of restoring old manor-houses with which English architecture of the fifteenth and sixteenth centuries have so richly endowed us. Many of these are as secluded as ever, and their atmosphere remains much the same as it originally was. The function of the National Trust under His Majesty's Office of Works is an investment the return on which is not only inestimable in tangible form, but will bear fruit in the growing realization of the greatness of the past and the urge towards maintaining that greatness in the future. Tattershall, Leeds, Allington, Caerphilly, Hurstmonceaux, and Bodiam are only a few examples of restoration for which the nation must be grateful. Yet how many others there are whose fortunes are waiting to be taken in hand and restored to something of their old grandeur, something of their old completeness, which the studied care of the expert can replace.

In this era of feverish building activity through which we are passing, how many really great works will stand out in the future as masterpieces of twentieth-century architecture? Is there any definite form emerging which will mark our period as one of enlightened architectural achievement in the annals of civilization? In this age of relative prosperity, what monuments are we raising to our own glory, even if the number and magnificence of the churches given us by our forebears precludes our building to the greater glory of God? For instance, what is the dominating motive in modern municipal building of recent years that will definitely bear the mark of the early twentieth century? The answer to these questions may lie in such buildings as Liverpool Cathedral and some of the recent municipal buildings in our great cities. Or it may be that the new architecture is still struggling towards enlightenment through a transitional period which as yet throws no clear-cut shadow on the screen.

Let us remember, in an age when democracy (save in our own country) is being harassed on all sides, that the world's finest compositions have been democratically conceived, and that if democracy in architecture is going to continue to find representative expression, it is the people who must be educated in what they want, so that their builders may carry out that expression. It is greater familiarity with what is that imparts the knowledge of what should be and the understanding of the difference between good and bad in design. It remains only for the eye to be opened to a proper sense of form and beauty. Democracy must speak with no uncertain voice in the planning of our great social housing schemes. Only by planning can it compare favourably with the efforts of the Fascist régime in Rome or that of any other great national movement of the present time. Hideous areas may be turned into vast new limbs of our largest cities to house the ever-growing urban population. And above all, let us see to it that while modern architecture is finding its feet in the mass of new building of to-day, we do not allow to fall into decay the beauties of yesterday, but help restoration to proceed side by side with modern construction.

What a tragedy it is that the awakening to a sense of

beauty in architecture, as to every aesthetic sense, comes
so long after a revolution, whether social or economic.
The history of the last century is repeating itself to-day.
How much bad building and absence of planning has to
be endured before the lesson is learnt and we begin to see
the necessity for starting aright!

Regarding the rapid spread of the towns that grew out
of the Industrial Revolution in the early nineteenth century, and stressing the inadequate accommodation and
the complete absence of order, Trevelyan again says:

'Town planning and any effort to brighten or embellish the
face of the street were alien to the ideas of the age. The enter-
prising employer wanted dwellings where the new hands he
wished to employ could live. The builder looked to make
money on the transaction. No one else gave the matter a
thought. Thus was the new England built.'

Much the same comment can be applied to-day.

It is for the future historian to present a well-balanced
account of the facts and to weigh the importance of events
in determining the stage which has been arrived at. There
is little doubt he will give due weight to the influence of
the great social revolution of the twentieth century. One
aspect of this revolution has here been introduced, if only
because of the alarming rapidity with which the encroachment of the town appears to be swallowing up the
country. It is the desire to engender respect and love for
the country which forms the *raison d'être* of this book, and
the effort that is necessary to be made by those who are
still fortunate enough to possess estates which their predecessors have kept up and done all in their power to
preserve and to beautify. So many famous and historic
places have been in the market in the last two decades
that we cannot but have suffered the inevitable loss which
occurs when the continuity of years of possession is
broken. Family records are lost or hidden away, and their
glamour does not long survive in the memory of local
tradition. The desirability of the family being able to go
on living in their own place, lavishing the care and love

on their houses out of an inbred sense of devotion, must be preferable, from the nation's point of view, to their being forced to sell their estates, even though a benevolent and paternal government department is prepared to take over some historical properties and preserve them for the benefit of posterity.

There are many who own priceless possessions, whether of simple beauty or national importance, and have not the means to restore. By restoration we mean essentially the catching up with arrears of decay not timely dealt with by a contemporary generation. It may mean the building up of that which has crumbled away beyond repair, using the best data available, or, failing such data, reconstructing with the best advice aided by imagination. But if their owners would record what they know about their possessions, England would be the richer, and by doing so they would be acknowledging a duty in handing down to posterity something to enable it to continue or complete the work of restoring them.

The foreground of this book is of little consequence. We have taken the reader back from the country-side of the present day, and, after duly stressing the need of putting forth an effort in the interests of its beauty, we set him down in an English village four hundred years ago. The centre is a manor-house that has passed through many vicissitudes under its respective owners.

The background consists of the constant changes in the country-side and the conditions in which the squire has waxed and waned, the events that have passed over him, together with the developments affecting him through four hundred years. *A Manor through Four Centuries* is therefore an attempt to set something on record lest it should be lost through the lapse of time. If, as we venture to hope, it acts as an inducement to owners of historical places of far greater importance than Roydon to make some account available for the nation's archaeologia, should they not already have done so, it will have served a further purpose.

CHAPTER II

PECKHAM: THE PARISH, THE MANOR, AND THE CHURCH

ROYDON, in the parish of East Peckham, lies on the western slopes of the hill known as Sir William's Hill, named after William Twysden. It has a view to the west and to the south across the River Medway, over the Weald and beyond. Its farm-lands consist of much that appertained to the original property, including the manors of Stokenbury and Lomewood in the adjoining parish of Nettlested. Its tenants, as in times gone by, still grow their fruit and hops down to the river, whose riparian pastures from time immemorial have been recognized as some of the richest grazing in Kent. It is a well-known saying that 'Land in sight of East Peckham Church is always worth £— an acre', and there is much land in sight of it—some of the richest and best in the garden of England.

Adjoining the nearby parish of East Farleigh is Stokenbury, a 'borough' lying to the south-east of Roydon. It was originally granted by the Conqueror to Cardinal Odo, Bishop of Baieux, as part of his possessions, but after the cardinal's banishment and disgrace the lands were freed by the confiscation of his property to the Crown, and were granted at the time of Bishop Lanfranc's consecration, four years after the Domesday Survey, to the Convent of Christchurch, Canterbury.

Lomewood was a part of Stokenbury and derived its name from the soil. The *Loam* or clay in which it abounds is especially suitable for making the best red-bricks, and these have in fact been made on this manor for many generations and are still being made to-day.

According to Phillipot, Lomewood belonged formerly to a Cloister of Black Canons in Oxford, dedicated to

St. Friswith, which was supported by Cardinal Wolsey in 1525 when he intended to erect the magnificent fabric of the College of Christ Church.

'The Manor was resigned to the Crown and was granted by King Henry VIII in the twenty-seventh year of his reign to Sr. Edward Nevill, who gave it in marriage, with his daughter Katherine Nevill, to John Roydon Esq., son of Thomas Roydon of Roydon Hall in Great Peckham, who determining in Elizabeth Roydon, his sole heir, she, by marrying William Twysden Esq., planted it into his revenue.'

The village of East Peckham and the ancient church are so closely associated with Roydon and its families that some account of them must be given in order to appreciate Roydon in its proper atmosphere and setting.

Peckham (from the Saxon 'Peac', a hill) came to be defined as a parish some twelve centuries ago, when Archbishop Theodore (A.D. 668–93), having formed the larger parishes into dioceses, began to establish the small parishes within them. A parish was originally an ecclesiastical division which owed its formation to the Church acting in conjunction with the large landowners in its locality. Not until the early seventeenth century did the civil parish gain recognition, and it usually became coterminous in the matter of jurisdiction with the older ecclesiastical parish.

Hasted records the earliest mention of Peckham in A.D. 961, 'When in this year Queen Edgiva, mother of King Edmund and King Eadred, gave for the healthe of her soul to Christchurch in Canterbury, this estate of Peckham.' Gervase, the Chronicler of Canterbury (*circa* 1190), records that it was during the reign of Edmund that the Queen Mother made this gift which had remained in her own right to bestow. As Edmund only reigned for six years (from A.D. 940 to 946) the grant, according to Gervase, would have been made between these two dates and therefore earlier than the year 961 accredited to it by Hasted. Phillipot, whom we shall quote again presently, placed it precisely in 941.

In 1070, the year of Archbishop Lanfranc's consecration, Peckham was still vested in Christchurch, when the revenues of this estate were enjoyed as one common stock by the archbishop and his convent. After the example of foreign churches, however, Lanfranc divided the lands of the archbishopric into two parts: the one for the maintenance of himself and his successors in the see of Canterbury; the other for his monks. In this partition Peckham fell to the lot of the monks for their subsistence and clothing (De Cibo aut de Vestitute monarchorum), and it is entered in Domesday (Pecheham) under the title of 'Terra Monarchorum Archiepi', or the land of the archbishop's monks. Queen Edgiva, widow of Edward (the Elder), thus established an interesting link with East Peckham which Canterbury still possesses after a lapse of nearly a thousand years. She was buried in the foundations of the ancient Saxon Cathedral of Canterbury, destroyed by fire in 1174.

Upon Crowhurst Farm there is 'Castle Field', probably so named after Ricard de Clare, Earl of Gloucester and Hereford, Knight of Tonbridge Castle, for it is recorded in Domesday that he owned land in Peckham, 450 acres and some woodland, granted to him by William the Conqueror in return for defending the lands of the Church. The Knights were charged with the duty of protecting the property of the monks in addition to their own, and at the time of Domesday this liability, so far as Peckham was concerned, was vested in Richard de Tonbridge. He was therefore rewarded with the Knight's Manor and may be said to have been the first Lord of the Manor of Great, or, as we know it, East Peckham. An even more prominent Kentish lord was Gundulph, Bishop of Rochester, builder of Rochester Cathedral and Castle and founder of the Abbey of Benedictine Nuns, dedicated to the Blessed Virgin Mary at Malling in A.D. 1090, the fourth year of William Rufus.

On the outskirts of this town, four miles distant from East Peckham, is Gundulph's Tower and Keep, a relic of a one-time stronghold, and reminiscent of the mighty sway the great baron-bishop held over this part of Kent. Raised ostensibly to protect the convent, it also formed an outpost and connecting link between Rochester and Tonbridge Castle, where his brother knight held almost equal power. We may easily imagine the retinues and wealth of these two great lords of the Medway Valley, with their resounding names, William de Gundulph and Richard de Tonbridge.[1]

Peckham had an interesting link with Rochester. The bridge over the Medway there has from the earliest times been famous for its importance, and although first mentioned only in the reign of Henry I, it probably existed long before then. Bishop Ernulf in 1115 issued regulations for the repair of Rochester Bridge, seemingly an ancient custom in his day. Different parties were responsible for the various piers. 'The fifth Pier is the Archbishop's, and he ought to plank four virgates and to lay three sills and this he ought to do from his lands of . . .', and here follows a register of thirteen parishes including that of Great Peckham. This appears to have been a periodical imposition upon the manor, and later, when a new bridge was built, Peckham had to contribute towards the cost of its erection.

Peckham was charged with another heavy obligation also, that of repairing the bridges over the Medway within its own parish boundaries. Certain areas of land, such as Bridge Croft, consisting of 2½ acres, was rented to the

---

[1] In the tenth year of King Edward II, the Prior of Canterbury obtained a charter of free warren for his Manor of Peckham, at which time the manor was valued at ten pounds a year.

Anno 38 *Henry III* (1253/4) 'at the Kent Assessments on the occasion of the Knighting of the Black Prince, Magna Peckham and West Peckham in the Hundred of *Littlefelde* are mentioned, and amongst other Feeholders at this time in the Hundred of Littlefelde are recorded Johannes de West Pecham and Willelmus de Mereworth.' (From the Charter Rolls.)

East Peckham Parish Records: 'The Right of Free Warren was granted over the demesne lands of Peckham to the Prior and Convent of Canterbury, by King Edward III in the thirty-eighth year of his reign, out of devotion to St. Thomas, the Martyr (1365), i.e. The Right to enclose and make a park, to hunt and to shoot game, other than DEER which was a separate right under the grant of FREE FORESTRY.'

Sovereign at an annual fee for keeping up the bridge above Yalding. Sir Roger Twysden records that in the reign of Charles I Bridge Croft formerly found 'Clappers' along the parish highway 'Up to a Great Oak there, standing some six Rods, and that although the borough of Stokenbury had not been charged with it, as much was taken out of the rent of the land as had been sufficient for making the road thither'.

Phillipot, the seventeenth-century county historian, in his 'Survey of Kent' (*Villare Cantianum*) gives the following account:

'Peckham in the Hundred of Twyford and Littlefield is distinguished from the other, first by its bulk and dimension, this being commonly called Great Peckham and then, second, by its situation, being styled in Records East Peckham. It was given to the Church of the Trinity, that is Christchurch in Canterbury, by Queen Ediva to the monks of that Convent, "ad Cibum" for a support of their diet and alimony, in the year of grace 941 and if you will see how it was rated in the Great Register of Domesday Book, take here a view of it.

'"Peckham", says that Record, "Temp Edwardi Regis se defendebat Pro VI Sallings" &c. Peckham in the time of Edward the Confessor "went for 7 Plough Lands" and defends itself now (temp. the Conqueror) after the same estimate, and was rated upon the appraisement formerly at 12 lbs., but now it is stated at 8. And thus regulated, was it for many years fastened to the patrimony of the Church, until the dissolution in the reign of Henry VIII, unloosened the cement, in the twenty-ninth year of that Prince, who afterwards about the thirty-sixth year of his reign grants this and divers other parcels of the Church Demesne to Sir Thomas Wyatt, who not long after, by Livery and Seisin, passes away his right in it to George Moulton Esq., but because there was a fine and recovery wanting, the sale was imperfect, so that he had it only in abeience (as the law stiles it) or in expectance. So that the Crown in the Second of Queen Mary, upon the defection and attaint of Sir Thomas Wyatt, finding this in the Tenure of Moulton, seized upon it as parcel of Wyatt's estate because it had not been before legally conveyed. And here it rested until Queen Elizabeth in the second year of her reign granted it to Anthony

Weldon Esq., one of the Justices of Peace in this county under the reign of Queen Mary, at which time he became eminent, by his vigorous opposing Sir Thomas Wyatt in that design he was then embarked in; and in this family (though not without some strugglings and contests at law about the title) did the Title reside until that age we stile *"Ours*, when it was conveyed to George Whetenhall Esq., who dying without issue, it came by descent to own for prop^n. Thomas Whetenhall, now of Great Peckham, Esq."

'But the Manor of East Peckham itself (as distinct from the Fee) rested in the Crown until the State, upon the death of the late King Charles (I 1649), granted it to Colonel Robert Gibbins.'[1]

It was at this time assessed by a survey at an annual value of £17.[2]

'The Court Lodge with the Demesne Lands of the Manor of East Peckham was granted the next year after the attainder of Sir Thomas Wyatt by Letters patent, anno 1st. and 2nd. King Philip and Queen Mary, to Sir John Baker to hold *in capite* by Knight's Service, who passed his interest in them in the second year of Queen Elizabeth to Anthony Weldon Esq., but the Crown afterwards disputing his title to them, the Queen in her tenth year granted them to William Dodington, and the next year the Attorney-General exhibited an information against the heirs of Weldon in the Court of Exchequer on account of these premises and judgment was had against him. After which a writ of error was brought and divers other law proceedings had, by which however at last, Ralph, son of Anthony Weldon above mentioned, established his title to them, and his son Sir Anthony Weldon in the latter end of the reign of King James I passed them away by sale to George Whetenhall Esq., after whose death they came by descent into the possession of Thomas Whetenhall Esq., of Hextall's Court in this Parish, whose descendant Henry Whetenhall Esq., alienated this estate to Sir William Twysden Bt. of Roydon Hall, whose descendant Sir Wm. Jarvis Twysden Bt. is the present possessor of it.'[3]

---

[1] Probably of the Parliament Party. He only held the title for a short time, and by the Restoration it was vested in Sir Roger Twysden.

[2] Hasted's *History of Kent* (vol. v, p. 94, 1782 edn.).

[3] It is interesting to note that the accounts of the two historians differ in some

Peckham was associated with the Insurrection of Jack Cade in 1450 through the enthusiasm of a then prominent local squire, William Hextall of Hextall's Place, some mention of whose family will be made later. This gentleman raised a contingent of East Peckham men and set out at their head to join the rebellion at Wrotham. The origin of Cade, its hero, is obscure and much uncertainty exists as to where he hailed from; Sussex Heathfield and Kentish Smarden lay equally ardent claim to having fostered him. The centre of the rising, to judge by the names mentioned in the Register of Pardons, was almost certainly Ashford. The ostensible cause of it lay—as the historians would have us believe—in the preferment of the men of Kent for the Duke of York, whose eldest son was later to become Edward IV. Cade is dubbed a 'rebellious imposter pretending to be John Mortimer of Royal Blood', and in support of this malediction is quoted the fact that he sought by violent means to establish a claim to the throne. Shakespeare in *King Henry the Sixth* (*Part 2*) rather naturally portrays Cade as a self-seeking impostor and his supporters as a low-class rabble.

It is, however, much more probable that some of the ancient customs and privileges of Kent and its neighbouring shires were threatened and that the misdirection of justice administered by the knights and sheriffs, appointed through favouritism from outside the county, may have been the instigating cause. Heavy and unjust extortion was practised by those in high authority, not excluding some members of the King's own Privy Council, to the exasperation of many good yeomen and craftsmen of the Weald and their brotherhood in the hinterland of the Cinque Ports. If the nature of the rising and the personnel supporting it be examined, evidence of which lies in the register of persons who later received the Royal Pardon, we cannot help being impressed with the large numbers

respects and must therefore be treated as being supplementary to one another. Hasted, whose *History of Kent* was published in 1782, a hundred years or more later than Phillipot, was contemporary with Sir William Jarvis Twysden of Roydon, mentioned above. He succeeded his father, the sixth baronet, in 1767.

of those of a highly respectable class who had allied themselves to the cause, whatever the pretext, presumably because their livelihood was menaced. Of knights there was but one—Sir John Cheyne of East Church, Sheppey. Only eighteen squires are recorded, of whom William Hextall of East Peckham is worthy of mention since the heiress of his family married William Whetenhall a century later. Among the seventy-four gentlemen named it is not surprising to find Roger Twysden of Great Chart near Ashford, the ancestor of the family that later came to live at Roydon. The remainder were yeomen and craftsmen who joined the rebellion in very large numbers.

Mr. Durrant Cooper,[1] who made an extensive study of the subject, says:

'It was not a disorganized mob, nor a chance gathering. In several Hundreds the Constables duly, and as if legally, summoned the men; . . . many parishes, particularly Marden, Penshurst (which belonged to the exiled Duke of Buckingham), Hawkhurst, Northfleet, Boughton-Malherbe, Smarden and Pluckley, furnished as many men as could be found in our own day fit for arms.'

Cade is designated John Mortimer in his pardon, dated Monday, July 6th, 1450, as appears by the Patent Roll, on the very day of the negotiations. Kent had been discontented in the early part of 1450, and Thomas Cheyney, a fuller of Canterbury 'calling himself an Heremite, yclepped *Blewberd*', had been arrested there on February 9th for raising a rebellion. He was executed and his head ordered to be sent into the city, but so great was his popularity that no one could be found sufficiently brave to take it there.

Cade's Insurrection of the Commons of Kent properly began at Blackheath (that convenient rallying-place) on Whit-Monday, June 1st, 1450. The King himself actually set out to subdue them, but found that they had fallen back upon Sevenoaks, whither, thinking easily to rout a disorderly mob, the brothers Stafford pursued them with an inadequate number of men and found the insurgents

[1] 'John Cade's followers in Kent', W. D. Cooper, F.S.A., 1869.

more formidable than he expected. They were beaten and slain almost to a man. The King, being advised that this was no ordinary rising, withdrew to his fortress of Kenilworth, while Cade was reinforced by strong contingents from the Sussex and Surrey borders. On July 3rd they entered the City of London, where they were joined by further supporters from the Essex side of the river. A short but vigorous battle was fought step by step from London Bridge to Smithfield. Although the action was uncertain in its result—few street engagements were ever otherwise—the citizens of London, fearing further loss of life and destruction of property, pressed the authorities to negotiate with Cade. There seems to have been some order and moderation on the side of the rebels, for the fighting was soon discontinued. Cade demanded the presentation of a 'Bill of Petitions' to the King by Kempe, the Lord Chancellor, and Waynflete, the Lord Bishop of Winchester, containing a general promise of redress and a charter of pardon to all the insurgents upon their agreeing to disperse quietly to their homes. The first clause in the petition stated that 'It is openly feared that Kent should be destroyed with Royal power and made a wild Forest, for the death of the Earl of Suffolk, of which the Commons were never guilty'.

Over-taxation and unjust levies in the area of the Cinque Ports, together with the denial of the right to elect their own knights of the shire, may have been the chief contributory causes of the rebellion, and the 20,000 partisans that Kent raised were mainly an earnest and respectable body of men. Although their leader was outlawed in spite of his pardon and slain soon after the rising, the result was a useful and salutary warning to the King and his Lords not to choose Kent in which to abuse the privileges of his subjects.

Returning to Peckham, the most important factor in tracing its development is the interesting medieval church. This church, dedicated to St. Michael, stands at the southern end of what is now a finely timbered wood but in olden days was known as 'Peckham Fyldes'. The site was admirably chosen, for the view looks right over Roydon and beyond the Weald itself. Domesday records in 1085 that at Peckham 'A church is there', and probably from the earliest Saxon times there was at the top of the 'peac' a rude little place of worship built of rough stone and wood. On this hill too, within the boundaries of the little church, was the early Christian burial-ground, while the mound or toll on Sir William's Hill, a mile distant, was more than likely the pagan burial-place since centuries before.

The ancient road which passes close to the church was used frequently by travellers and pilgrims journeying from west Kent via Maidstone[1] to join the main Pilgrim's Way to Canterbury beyond it.

Textus Roffensis, the Chronicle of Rochester, was not compiled until about 1115, but it records the doings of the great Gundulph, Bishop of Rochester, previously referred to, who in 1089 reorganized the levies in the benefice, and that Peckham was bound to pay every Easter 9*d.* 'Chrism Fee' for the baptismal oil—the oil blessed by the bishop for anointing. Gundulph was not the first to institute the Chrism Fee, but it was he who revised the early method of paying tithe in some kind (e.g. in the form of a sheep or a cheese) and substituted a regular money payment instead. The entry no doubt was recorded when the old Saxon church was still surviving, as it is unlikely that a new church had been built so soon after the Conquest or that the ancient church would yet have been dedicated to a Christian saint.

Security in the eleventh and twelfth centuries took precedence generally over religious improvement in the matter of building. Most of the master-masons and builders not regularly employed by the King or the great ecclesiastical bodies and wealthy monasteries were engaged in erecting castles to the order of the barons. The tem-

---

[1] Roman, *Vagniacae*; Saxon, *Medwegston.*

porary interruption in church building caused by secular building partly accounts for the fact that Norman architecture is less abundantly represented among our country churches than the 'Early English' and 'Decorated' periods, which followed afterwards in more peaceful times.

Although it was not until 1318 that Martin de Beauvais was installed first vicar of Peckham, it is safe to infer that the church was erected and established as a place of worship at a much earlier date with a 'visitor' appointed by Christchurch.

It is probable also, to judge by the long intervals between construction, particularly in the thirteenth- and fourteenth-century work, that the church was never completed as it was originally planned and that the progress of building was interrupted, if not marred, on at least one occasion by important historical events. These exercised their influence over church building not only throughout the see of Canterbury but considerably beyond its boundaries.

As to whether Peckham was especially favoured or not, one has to see the magnificent site upon which the church stands to appreciate why it may have been singled out to possess a monumental building. It is sad to meditate upon the church that might have been there had it not been for the events that interfered with its construction.

St. Michael's began to be raised at the expense of the Prior and Convent of Christchurch during the latter half of the twelfth century, by which time the endowments granted to that great ecclesiastical body had already blessed it with much wealth. It is a tribute to Peckham that the parish was considered sufficiently important in the see for its church to be named after St. Michael, who was wont to receive special veneration at Canterbury Cathedral, where a chapel had long been dedicated to him.

Owing to the too drastic treatment, twenty-five years ago, to the exterior of the church in a worthy attempt to arrest the deterioration of the fabric, some of the most reliable data from which to arrive at the commencement and evolution of its building are no longer available. The entire north wall of the nave and three sides of the square tower were covered with a thick overlay of stucco, and not until this peels off with the process of time will those portions be revealed once again to become a problem to the curators of the church in future generations. But their concealment gives rise to the question whether or not the nave is contemporary with the chancel, the north wall of which, remaining uncovered, is, as far as can now be seen, the earliest part of the church.

The chancel is definitely of Norman character, for it includes a small single light close to the extreme east end of the wall.

Behind the stucco on the exterior of the nave lies the important evidence that the line of the base course, together with the materials in it, could supply to help to determine the later treatment of the whole plan of the nave and tower, if it were to become visible. One is forced, therefore, to make the remaining deductions from the inside of the church. Taking a compass bearing, first in the nave and then in the chancel, it will be found that the nave lies several degrees north of true east and that the chancel north wall and arcade are still farther out of alinement. Moreover, the two easternmost arcades of the nave are of the earlier character, suggesting the Norman or subsequent transitional style before entering upon the Early English. At the second pillar, opposite the vestry steps, the arches change into the less massive structure of the later period, which fact suggests that it has been continued, or possibly the whole nave reconstructed, at a later date.

'It is a frequent source of error to assume that the church originally consisted of a nave only, or a chancel without a nave. It was not the custom to build portions of churches and leave the completion to future generations.'[1] Nevertheless, there may have been for some very good reason a cessation of work at a point where the

---

[1] *Medieval Styles of the English Parish Church*, by F. E. Howard.

structure of Peckham Church was sufficiently adequate for the services of the parish without the fullness of its completion yet having been realized.

It is more than probable that the church was rebuilt late in the twelfth century, when it consisted of a chancel, a nave, and possibly a small south aisle, and was continued until its building had arrived at the second column of the arcade already referred to. At this juncture some exterior event seems to have occurred to cause a cessation of work, and it is necessary to cast round for a possible cause. This is likely to have been the blow suffered by the see in the fire which destroyed the old Saxon Cathedral of Canterbury. Thomas à Beckett was murdered in 1170, and four years later Canterbury Cathedral was burnt to the ground; a fact that, whether it was significant as a just retribution or not, Christendom must be thankful for in the glorious building that began almost immediately to take its place. Throughout the thirteenth century wealth was poured into Christchurch abundantly by the pilgrims visiting the shrine of the martyred archbishop, and their alms were readily given to help the noble pile of the great new cathedral that they saw rising before their eyes. By the latter half of this century so much had been contributed that not only was the completion of the edifice assured, but much remained over for the see to spend by way of enlarging and beautifying the churches in its outlying parishes.

If it be assumed that St. Michael's had reached the first stage of its building at the time when old Saxon Canterbury was reduced to ruins, it may be concluded without much doubt that Peckham was one of those parishes favoured with a resumption of work towards the end of the thirteenth century, either by way of continuing or by reconstructing the existing church. The nave was carried to its full length by the addition of two more arcades, and early in the fourteenth century the tower was built to complete the length of the structure. The east wall of the chancel was rebuilt and the chancel aisle added in the

latter half of the fourteenth century. This was dedicated
to the Blessed Virgin Mary as the Chantry Chapel of St.
Mary, in which it was the custom to hold special prayers
and sing masses for the souls of the departed monks of
Christchurch. Late in the fifteenth century a fine perpendicular window was inserted near the eastern end of
the south wall of the chancel aisle, probably to light a
new reredos, and in the seventeenth century the chapel
was taken over as a mortuary chapel by the Twysden
family. Its upkeep has devolved upon the owner of
Roydon Hall to this day.

A long interval elapsed from about 1320 until well into
the fifteenth century, when another interruption in the
course of building seems to have occurred and a second
question arises as to whether St. Michael's was not again
the victim of unlucky circumstances just at a time when a
considerable outlay was planned for enlarging the church.
In 1348 the Black Death smote the country with a heavy
hand and brought about the curtailment far and wide of
anything in the nature of extravagant building enterprise.
On the outbreak of the Plague in 1348, the incumbent,
William, dictus de Walys, who was installed in 1325, died
or fled for fear of the scourge, and in 1349 a new vicar,
John de Lichfield, was appointed.[1] The sudden ravages
of the Black Death cut off like a knife the activities of
enlarging and beautifying the churches, and all plans were
left in abeyance to be finished as and when it was practicable, any elaborate designs being accordingly curtailed.
The riches of the see of Canterbury were diverted to the
more humane purpose of relieving distress within its
parochial jurisdiction.

It was not until the fifteenth century that work upon
St. Michael's was resumed, and by its close the church
looked very much as it does to-day. During the final
stage of its completion the main aisle was rebuilt and
widened to the south, the large windows being ornamented with tracery of the contemporary period. The

[1] For List of Incumbents see note at end of chapter, p. 31.

whole church was re-roofed in timber covered with tiles, the high-pitched king-posts employed being common to that time and found in many churches throughout south-east England. On the conclusion of this work the porch was added by way of a final feature. Much of the early tinted glass remains, but Peckham cannot boast the beautiful old glass that belongs to its near neighbour at Nettlested.

The parish register records how various benefactors left money to be spent on finishing and decorating the church. For instance, in 1420 one John Mew requested that he might be buried in the Chapel of St. Mary and left a sum for decorating the fabric of the chancel. In 1491 John Cayzer[1] bequeathed a considerable amount for the construction of two windows in the tower and the making of a south window to St. Blayzius (the patron saint of Wool). This gentleman was no doubt a prosperous Kentish wool-grower. Ralph Brokar in 1507 left six marks to the church porch. It is not therefore surprising to find that the porch is of a later style suggesting the perpendicular, as also are the windows of the tower. The many gifts recorded, with their dates, make it plain that the adornment of the church continued intermittently throughout the fifteenth and early sixteenth centuries.

A sidelight on the process of building in early Norman times has been collected from the church records by the present vicar.

'The architect of the church was the Master-Mason. The first thing to be done was to pull down the little old Saxon Church and use its stone materials for the foundations of the new edifice; then he had to order the opening of a stone-quarry (there are traces of this within 100 yards north-west of the Tower) and arrange for bringing up the Rag-stone. A lodge was set up as a work shop for the stone-carvers, the lodge being roughly built of timber with sleeping accommodation above. There were freemasons and rough-masons who usually wore gloves at their work. The rates of pay were 5*d*

---

[1] John Cayzer also bequeathed the sum of 5*s*. yearly for three years to be spent on herrings for the poor people on the first day of Lent. In those days meat was strictly forbidden during Lent.

a day in summer, 4*d* in spring and autumn and 3*d* in winter. Stone-cutting in a lodge was an unhealthy occupation, for the stone dust irritated the throat and consequently there was always a great shortage of masons. The King required large numbers of them for building castles and made the Sheriffs of the Counties supply him with men. The great Barons also attracted many of the skilled masons and there was competition in the rates of wages they paid as well as in the size and magnificence of their edifices. But the great majority of labourers required were mere hewers of wood and drawers of water; their wages if any were scanty and so the passion for building made the people poor at a time when otherwise England was prosperous.'

The church registers of the fifteenth century refer more than once to a rood, which shows that there was at least a beam (or 'perk') spanning the arch between the chancel and the nave. Upon this the rood or crucifix would be placed and there would be a special window to throw light upon it. The single light near the present pulpit suggests this as being likely, and there may even have been an oak screen of carved lattice-work with an altar in front and an aperture on either side leading into the chancel. If there was a loft also, it might have been used as a music gallery and would have been adequately lit by the same window. Although this is pure conjecture, it is probable that Peckham Church, like so many of its contemporaries, conformed to the requirements of those times, which were 'to provide for a comely partition betwixt your chancel and the body of the church, as required by Law'.

In the nave there is a fine brass, representing a worthy merchant with his wife, dressed in the period of about 1500. He was probably an alderman of the City of London, as he is depicted wearing 'Minever' or Squirrel's Fur, which is a sign of minor office. The subjects are almost certain to be William Whetenhall and his wife Margaret Hextall.

In a north window of the nave also there is an interesting inscription which reads, 'HERE STOODE THE WICKED

IMAGE [?] OF S. MYCHAEL A WAYING OF [SOULS?] BY THE
LAWE OF QUENE ELIZABETH (?) ACCORDING TO GOD['S
HOLY?] WORD IS TAKEN AWAYE.' The inscription in the
old glass obviously tells the story of one of the periodical
defacements that were all too common occurrences and
have spoiled many of our churches of their unique and
historical monuments. It is miraculous that any should
have survived the wholesale depredations of the zealots
of the Reformation and of the Puritan campaign during
the Commonwealth.[1]

There is a quaint story which throws some light on the
above reference and offers a possible explanation of the
particular significance of an image of St. Michael, always
assuming that it has nothing whatever to do with the
patron saint of the church. The early Coptic Christians
were loath to abandon their ancient pagan customs, and
one of their favourite beliefs was that Thoth weighed the
soul at death. Clinging firmly to this idea, they reconciled
it to their Christian faith by substituting the Archangel
Michael for Thoth. This no doubt came about in the
following manner. Early in the fourth century there
existed in the Temple of Saturn in Alexandria an idol of
brass named Michael, to whom sacrifices were regularly
offered. The bishop at that time, anxious to persuade the
Coptic Church to cease from idol-worship, suggested that
Michael the Archangel might take the place of Michael
the Idol. In consequence that idol was duly broken up

---

[1] *The Times*, Dec. 23rd, 1937: *Cromwell and Churches*. From the beginning of
the Long Parliament in 1640 Oliver 'was much hearkened to' (Sir Philip Warwick's Memoirs). Between 1640 and 1642 he attended 45 Committees, including
the Committee of Religion. On January 23, 1640–41, Rushworth records:
'That commissions be sent into all counties for the defacing, demolishing and
quite taking away all images, altars, or tables turned altar-wise, crucifixes, superstitious pictures, monuments and reliques of idolatry out of all churches and
chapels.' As Oliver was on the Committee of Religion the inference is that this
order met with his approval, and this conjecture finds confirmation in the report
of an eye-witness who was present when Cromwell visited Peterborough
Cathedral. After remarking that 'this Cromwell out-vied . . . that Cromwell of
Henry VIII time', he proceeds with an account of the destruction of the 'Great
West Window'. After witnessing more havoc Cromwell was asked that 'he would
please to stay his soldiers from further defacing and ruining that place. All the
satisfaction he could get was but a provocation to further mischief.'—Mr. E.
Verdon Paterson, Church View, South Harting, Petersfield, Hants.

and fashioned into a cross, and the Temple of Saturn became the church of St. Michael, and it is recorded by a tenth-century writer that 'The Copts in Egypt and Alexandria still keep the feast on that day (November 8th) to the Angel Michael and sacrifice numerous victims'. Whether or not the story has any foundation or whether it is too far a cry from Alexandria to East Peckham, the allusion to the image of Michael is too picturesque to be excluded.

In England ever since the introduction of Christianity images had their uses, and this fact was recognized even at the time of the Reformation. Not only the scarcity of books but the illiteracy of all but the higher orders required that some reminder in the prescribed form of a statue should assist those whose learning and religious qualities were deficient. Henry VIII allowed them to remain so long as they did not lead to idolatry, and so far as the parishioners of Peckham did not appear to have bowed the knee to their image, it did not incur the royal displeasure and destruction. Why then was it removed by the law of Queen Elizabeth?

There is a possible explanation. In the second year of her reign the Queen 'forbade it to extol the dignity of any image whatsoever', and although she issued a more explicit, if somewhat contradictory, proclamation in the following year warning all persons 'to forbear breaking or defacing any image or glass windows in churches', it is probable that some of her ministers were over-zealous in their manner of promoting the Protestant faith and lost no time in interpreting her first edict as an injunction to suppress all visible forms of worship. No doubt too they were happy to seize upon an excuse thus to deal another blow at Popery. The very fact that the Queen issued her second edict relating to images so soon after the first renders it likely that a great deal of vandalism quickly took place.

Even if our image had escaped this destruction, it is highly improbable it would have survived the much more virulent and widely distributed attacks of the Puritans in the seventeenth century. There are other signs of mutilation in the church which must be ascribed to this latter period. These were troublesome times indeed. An extract from the parish records in 1646 gives an idea of the state of unrest which prevailed during the Civil War:

'The True Copie of an order granted to some of the Parishioners of Brenchley[1] allowing John Topping, Minister of East Peckham powre to baptize their children. . . . Whereas complaints have often been made unto us by many of ye principall inhabitants of the Parish of Brenchley that they having desired Mr. Gilbert, Minister of the same parish to baptize their children; and according to ye Directorie[2] offered to present them before the Congregation, hee hath neglected or refused toe so doe. Whereby divers infants remaine unbaptized, some of them being about a year old: expresly contrarie to ye sayd Directorie. We do therefore order that ye parents of such children do bring them unto ye Parish Church of East Peckham upon a day. Where we desire that Mr. Topping, Minist^r of ye same Parish would baptize them according to ye sayd Directorie, they acquainting him with ye day they intend to bring them before hand.

Dated the 25th of May 1646.
JOHN SEDLEY.
JOHN RAYNEY.
ISAAC SEDLEY.'

In 1640 a complaint was lodged by the parishioners against their parson, the Reverend Ffrancis Worrall, on the grounds that he was not only vicar of East Peckham but also of Wateringbury, two miles distant from them.

'That the said Ffrancis Worrall doth many times serve the Cure himselfe of both these Parishes and is soe uncertayne at such tymes in officiating his cure that, our Parish being

---

[1] *Brenchley.* A neighbouring parish whose church is some seven miles to the south of St. Michael's, East Peckham.

[2] The Directory was the Order of Service foisted upon the people when the use of the Prayer Book was prohibited in 1645. Large numbers of the clergy refused to conform and loyal parsons protested in a number of practical ways of which the above is an example. Mr. Topping no doubt was one of Cromwell's temporary impositions, the rightful incumbent being Mr. Polhill, who may have been suspended for a similar reason (see p. 31).

spacious, the Parishioners cannot come to church with any convenience in the morning, and at other tymes (at tyme accustomed in other parishes) loste theire labour, he being dispatcht and gone to his Cure in Wateringbury. He is very negligent in preaching, insomuch that we have not a Sermon at our Parish above once in a fortnight (except it be a funerale Sermon which is very seldome).'

Evidently the parishioners of that time, unlike those of the present, could not have too much of a good thing in the way of sermons or funerals, and certainly were not inclined to regard the orations of their pastor as a burden, nor to let him off with anything less than one effusion weekly. They probably had strong suspicions that their brethren in Wateringbury were better served than they, for they pressed their cause strongly and procured its endorsement by Sir Edward Dering, the local Member of Parliament for Kent, who succeeded in evicting the unfortunate Mr. Worrall from the parish. In 1644 he was forced to retire on Wateringbury and make it his stronghold, where he remained unmolested until he died in 1652.

Here it may be mentioned that Sir Edward Dering was at that time taking a prominent part in ecclesiastical matters. He had brought in a Bill in Parliament for the 'Utter Abolition of Bishops' couched in somewhat violent terms. It must be assumed that this was too extreme a measure at the time to succeed, for the necessary support was not forthcoming and the Bill failed ignominiously. He published soon afterwards a book to the same effect, but the members of the House sat in judgement upon him for abusing a privilege and he was ejected from Parliament. His book was ordered to be burnt by the Common Hangman. He suffered a short imprisonment in the Tower, but in 1644 marched at the head of his troop of horse and was present at the unfurling of the Royal Standard at Nottingham. He died in the same year. Clarendon writes of him as 'A man of levity and vanity, easily flattered by being commended', but this may be unjust. He was jovial and popular and, perhaps, if his peculiar religious principles had not got the better of him, he would have carried enough respect in the county to have represented it throughout the Long Parliament.

In East Peckham Church lie the remains of those Roydons who originally gave their name to the place, and there are the tombs and monuments of Hextalls, Whetenhalls, and Twysdens, those of the latter being among the most beautiful of the memorial decorations.

In the English village from the earliest times life centred round the church, the manor, and its demesne. The village people themselves consisted mainly of those employed directly or indirectly by the lord of the manor, as we shall see in a later chapter. Suffice it to say that East Peckham was a typical, quiet, and mildly prosperous little community, such as was to be found all over England during this time and for many generations afterwards. Its population has varied very little in the last five hundred years.

Kent was one of the first counties to pursue cricket and may justly lay claim to a part in the parentage of the game. A certain letter is recorded from Viscount Sackville to his son Charles, dated at Pall Mall, June 17th, 1785:

'G. Damer went to the Cricket Match at Peckham and was much entertained at seeing old Cumberland directing all the players, and Charles acting first part in the game, but unfortunately Tunbridge lost the match and the only comfort the father had was that his boy had done his duty.'

Although no traces of the personalities referred to remain in East Peckham, the sentiment expressed was a very proper one and no doubt felt deeply at the time. Cricket from the beginning of its pursuit has been played in most villages in Kent, and cricket is still played in East Peckham on 'Parsons Meadow', the nearest approach to a level pitch (and that I regret to say far from level, as I have often experienced to my great discomfort) to be found within easy range of the squire, the parson, and the rest of the community, but this ground is only now equalled by the beautiful and (from the point of view of cricket) historical ground of the modern part of the village of East Peckham down by the river. This now has a family many times as great as its old parent on the top of the hill with its own church, schools, and social amenities, and may be considered now to all intents and purposes a separate parish.

LIST OF INCUMBENTS

The Reverend L. B. Larking (Curate of East Peckham from 1821 to 1830) gives the following record of Incumbents from the 15th century, in so far as he was able to derive their names and the dates of their incumbency from the manuscripts of Sir Roger Twysden, to which he became entitled (see note, pp. 91–2). The author has made one or two corrections and brought the list up to date.

Patrons		*Rectors*
Prior and Convent of Christ Church, Canterbury	—	William Bansor.
	1420	Richard Etclesley (ob. 1426).
	1474	John Dorant.
	1530	Thomas Bedell.
	1536	Thomas Mercer.
		Vicars
	—	John Tomson.
	1534	John Chamber.
1539. The King (at the Dissolution of the Priory of Christ Church, Canterbury).		
1541. Dean and Chapter of Canterbury (by Dotation Charter of Henry VIII).		
	1574	Nicholas Gyer.
	1611	— Richards.
	1616	Francis Worrall (ejected 1644; also Vicar of Wateringbury[1]).
	1644	William F. Polhill.
	1646	John Topping (appointed by the Parliament).
	1661	Samuel Grymes (formerly Vicar of Hadlow).
	1664	Richard Marsh.
	1689	Valentine Chadwick.
	1719	William Bradshaw (Prebendary of Canterbury and afterwards Bishop of Bristol).
	1722	John Hedges.

[1] See p. 28.

Patrons		*Vicars*
Dean and Chapter of Canterbury	1751	Francis Walwin (Preb. of Cant.; also Rector of St. Mary Bredman, Cant.).
	1758	Henry Hall (Librarian to the Archbp., also Rector of Harbledown and of Orpington; Treasurer of Wells Cathedral).
	1763	John Davis (Preb. of Cant.; also Rector of Hamsey in the county of Sussex).
	1766	William Tatton (Preb. of Cant.; also Rector of Rotherfield).
	1775	George Berkeley (Preb. of Cant.; also Vicar of Cookham in the county of Berks.).
	—	— Lucas.
	—	Thomas Vyner (Preb. of Cant.).
	1807	George Moore (Preb. of Cant.; also Rector of Wrotham cum Stansted).
	1853	Middleton Onslow.
	1884	Henry Robert Merewether.
	1900	Philip Wood Loosemoor.
	1911	Geoffrey Charles Edward Ryley (Hon. Canon of Rochester).
	1929	A. H. Partridge.
	1934	F. W. Bennitt.

Hic iacet dũs Ricardus Etclesley quondam Rector
Istius ecclesie qui obijt xx die mensis maij Anno
dũi mℓ CCCC xxbj cuius aïe propicietur deus Amen

RICHARD ETCLESLEY

Drawing of a Monumental brass that used to be in Peckham Church. The inscription is on the floor of the Chancel, immediately outside the Altar Rails, but the figure has been removed.

Etclesley was also a monk of Canterbury and was Rector of Peckham for 14 years until he died in 1426. He has the Monk's tonsure and is dressed in a long surplice with sleeves over which he wears an almuce of grey fur, a sign of dignity and a privilege much valued by the wearer. In this case it is probable that he was favoured by the Archbishop for being a member of the Chapter of Canterbury.

Although the priest is holding a chalice in his hands, the Robes are not those worn for celebrating Mass, but more probably are processional vestments. Chalices were frequently buried with the Clergy. In 1230 the Bishop of Winchester ordered that an unconsecrated vessel of tin or other base metal be provided in every church of the Diocese for burial with the parish priest.

Richard Etclesley left in his will a gilt chalice to Peckham Church and desired that he should be buried in the Chancel. The original brass figure on his tombstone was 2 ft. 7 in. in length and 10 inches in breadth.

CHAPTER III

THREE PECKHAM FAMILIES

IN the reign of Richard the Second there came into Kent a gentleman of the name of Richard Hextal, whose family were of Hextal Manor in Staffordshire. He married Anne Grovehurst, a wealthy heiress whose father owned considerable property between Horsmonden and Peckham, and upon his father-in-law's death Richard Hextal by this alliance found his possessions in the county greatly increased. He had previously acquired some land in Peckham upon which he built his own house, naming it after himself, as was the custom when founding a branch of the family in a new locality. Hasted in the eighteenth century described the place as 'venerable for its antiquity'. In the old Manor Rolls it was designated 'Hextall's Court' and was 'The Mansion of Gentlemen of that name who were of no small account in these parts'.

Richard had a son William, previously alluded to as having taken part in the Kentish Rebellion of 1450, when he led a contingent of Peckhamites to join Jack Cade. He, together with many others, received the Royal Pardon and apparently became a prominent man in the county, for his name was highly respected and he owned lands in Kent as far afield as Chilham and Dover. Having no male heir at his death, he left his estates to his two daughters, the elder of whom, Jane, married Sir John Bromley, Kt., while the second, Margaret, married William Whetenhall[1]

[1] *Whetnal*. The Kent Archaeological Society gives an account of a letter written by Archbishop Warham to Wm. Whetnal of Hextalls, East Peckham. Warham was Archbishop of Canterbury in the time of Henry VII and VIII, and was a distinguished and capable man, but was eclipsed by Wolsey in his later days. The subject of the letter was a proposal to found a Grammar School for forty Scholars at Tunbridge as a preparation for Oxford. The site proposed was the ancient priory of Tunbridge (probably that of the Black Canons). The suggestion did not find favour with the people of that town and was endorsed as follows: 'The inhabytauntes of Tunbridge had rather theyre Pryory stode still than to have a schole for XL children, to be sent thence to Oxford.' So that was that, and the proposal was abandoned. The letter was addressed by the

the younger, son of William Whetenhall, Alderman of the City of London and lord of a manor called after his own name near Chester. Jane may have predeceased her sister or they may each have received their portion upon their father's death, but Hextal descended to Margaret and was carried by marriage into her husband's name. From the end of the fifteenth century it became the seat of that branch of the Whetenhall family for many generations afterwards, until in the eighteenth century it was alienated to John Fane, Earl of Westmorland. He died without issue in 1762 and left it, together with his other estates in Kent, to his nephew Sir Francis Dashwood, who later became Lord le Despencer. This interesting barony, by virtue of the original creation by James I of Marie, Lady Fane, to be Baroness le Despencer in her own right, has more than once passed through the female line. By marriage to the Falmouth family in 1845 the property was conveyed to Viscount Falmouth and remains in the possession of the present holder of that title to this day.

Phillipot, in reference to certain manor grants in East, or Great Peckham, mentions 'Eastmere', a small property originally known as 'Remkin', being granted to William Hextal, per Margaret Hextal in the reign of King Henry VII. In the visitation of Kent for the purpose of verifying landowners and their titles in 1592, a century later, it is recorded in the parish registers: 'Whetenhall, Alderman of London, had issue William Whetenhall of East Peckham, who married Margaret, daughter and sole heir of William Hextal of East Peckham, and had issue George, Lewis and Margaret'. The latter married Thomas Roydon, whose family is the last of the three that we shall presently have to trace in forming the complete link with the Roydons.

The brass in the nave of Peckham Church represents

WILLIAM AND MARGARET WHETENHALL, 1539
Brass in the Nave, East Peckham Church

the above-mentioned William Whetenhall, who was sheriff of Kent in the eighteenth year of King Henry VIII's reign (1526), and his wife, formerly Margaret Hextal.

Hextal lay comfortably in the Weald below Roydon. The stream which flows past it fed the moat surrounding the house before proceeding to join the Medway above Yalding. The old mansion has long since fallen into decay and been pulled down. On its foundations a smaller building now stands called Peckham Place, and the present Hextal is an eighteenth-century house erected in the old pleasaunce a quarter of a mile from the site of the ancient demesne. The situation is about eleven miles from Tunbridge Wells and five from Somerhill, to which we shall presently refer.

It is well known that King Charles II loved to escape from the ennui of Whitehall in the summer to enjoy the lighter diversions of 'the Wells'. For the two hottest months of the year it was customary to arrange an informal recess for the Court, when those especial friends of the King, and a party selected carefully for their various talents, were invited to stay at the several fine houses in the neighbourhood.

Macaulay, describing Tunbridge Wells in 1685, writes:

'When the Court, soon after the Restoration, visited Tunbridge Wells, there was no town: but, within a mile of the Spring, rustic cottages, somewhat cleaner and neater than the ordinary cottages of that time, were scattered over the Heath. Some of these cabins were moveable, and were carried on sledges from one part of the common to another. To these huts men of fashion, wearied with the din and smoke of London, sometimes came in the summer to breathe fresh air, and to catch a glimpse of rural life. During the season a kind of fair was daily held near the fountain. The wives and daughters of the Kentish farmers came from the neighbouring villages with cream, cherries, wheatears, and quails. To chaffer with them, to flirt with them, to praise their straw hats and tight heels, was a refreshing pastime for voluptuaries sick of the airs of actresses and maids of Honour. Milliners, toymen, and jewellers came down from London, and opened a bazaar under the trees. In one booth the politician might find his coffee and the London Gazette; in another were gamblers playing deep at basset; and, on fine evenings, the fiddles were in attendance, and there were Morris Dances on the elastic turf of the bowling green.'

In this happy and informal atmosphere of relaxation the King was, according to the *Memoirs* of the Comte de Gramont,[1] staying upon one occasion 'with some select companions' at Somerhill, at that time the residence of Lord and Lady Muskerry.[2]

It is an amusing matter of conjecture as to whether Peckham can lay serious claim to be the scene of 'A Peckham Frolic, or Nell Gwyn'. This masque, as the title suggests, was an eighteenth-century caricature of the Merrie Monarch and his entourage in an episode connected with the Court. It was written by Edward Jerningham and published in 1779 after what must be presumed to have been a sufficiently delicate interval to satisfy the public taste without provoking the consequences of *lèse-majesté*. There is little doubt that the play was a 'best seller' of the time, for it included in its cast La Belle Stewart in addition to the two principal characters and most of the celebrated rakes of that interlude of easy morality that followed the Restoration. It was calculated to amuse the not too refined society of a hundred years later, when the gentler susceptibilities had more than ever to hide themselves beneath those outward and visible signs of mirth, which the fashion of the day required good breeding and good manners to countenance if not to approve. Rochester, the bane of all virtuous maidens, Tom Killigrew, Jermyn, and Charles Sedley of St. Clere, Ightham, the handsome doyen of Tunbridge Society, were each given a part in the play, which, if it was ever

---

[1] The popular French dilettante at the Court. *The Memoirs of the Comte de Gramont*, by Anthony Hamilton.

[2] She was the grotesque lady who gained the nickname of 'the Princess of Babylon' for her behaviour at one of the elaborate fancy-dress Balls held at the Court soon after the Restoration.

performed, was sure to have been successful from the promoters' point of view.

But if Peckham was the gay place chosen as the *mise en scène* of a frolic for those in high places, it was not always so, as is abundantly clear from the complaints of a certain young lady who was a favourite of the Comte de Gramont and his brother-in-law George Hamilton. It is this lady whose adventure, cut short by an untimely and unhappy demise, affords an interesting picture of the society of the time, and it may conceivably have been she who inspired the title of 'A Peckham Frolic'.

Elizabeth Bedingfield of Beckhal in Norfolk was related to the old Oxborough family of that name and to the celebrated Sir Thomas Bedingfield, who had the custody of Queen Elizabeth's royal person during her detention at Oxburgh in the reign of her elder sister. Miss Bedingfield was a very beautiful girl who, at the tender age of sixteen, married for some unaccountable reason Thomas Whetenhall of Hextal, soon after that worthy man had laid to rest his first wife when she had reached the mature age of sixty-three. It does not, however, follow that he himself was as old when he entered a second time upon matrimony. He appears to have been destined for the Church, for in his youth he had made a diligent study of theology, but on the death of his brother he gave up the project and settled down in the seat of his inheritance, there to pursue his bibliological studies in the somewhat incongruous atmosphere of partnership with an attractive young wife. Certainly he permitted himself the indulgence of a honeymoon in Paris, but it turned out to be mainly for the purpose of an expedition to the Rue St. Jacques, there to search for still more of those rare books with which to adorn the library at Hextal that formed his favourite pursuit. For Elizabeth, her home at Peckham was monotonous and uncongenial in the extreme—a misfortune that their ages and outlook upon life did nothing to relieve, for indeed these two could have had scarcely anything in common. The surroundings in which she lived were completely out of harmony with her enchanting disposition and she began to hunger after those pleasures with which, on account of the habits and pursuits of her husband, she was forced to go unsatisfied.

Hamilton declares that 'Mr. Whetenhall was all day long poring over his books and went to bed soon in order to rise early; so that his wife found him snoring when she came to bed, and when he rose he left her there sound asleep'—an unfair situation for a young lady of charm and virtue to find herself confronted with in such days as those which immediately followed the Restoration. Nor could Peckham by any stretch of the imagination claim to be gay and amusing, unless some happy chance had endowed it for one halcyon day to represent the scene of 'A Peckham Frolic'; in the opinion of Mrs. Whetenhall's friend 'The melancholy retired situation of the place was to her insupportable'. What more natural, therefore, that the young lady should, first reluctantly, then as time wore on, more eagerly, look for some diversion for a few harmless hours from the loneliness and boredom by which she was daily beleaguered? Hamilton continues:

'This had occasioned her to make some reflections, and then to reason upon those reflections; as for instance, that since her husband chose rather to devote himself to his studies, than to the duties of matrimony, to turn over musty old books, rather than attend to the attractions of beauty, and to gratify his own pleasures rather than those of his wife, it might be permitted her to relieve some necessitous lover, in neighbourly charity, provided she could do it conscientiously, and to direct her inclinations in so just a manner, that the evil spirit should have no concern in it.'

Elizabeth determined that in these matters Mr. Whetenhall should not be consulted, and having thus far shaped her destiny, turned to the friend who she knew could help her and who with womanly perception had taken pity upon her in the Rue St. Jacques. Miss Hamilton, sister to the biographer of the Comte de Gramont, and later to become that noble gentleman's wife, supported the aspirations of the unfortunate young Mrs. Wheten- hall and endeavoured to persuade her not to waste her time any longer in the sterile surroundings of Peckham, but immediately to pay her a long visit to London, where they would arrange a number of amusing parties and meet many of her interesting friends. When it came to the point of being unfaithful to her husband, Elizabeth's courage quite properly was lacking, and in days when such things were but lightly regarded, she found her powers to attract began to wane in direct proportion to her reluctance to gratify her lovers. There was a short and promising affair with George Hamilton, her friend's brother, which, for the reasons aforesaid, came to nothing, and 'soon after being obliged to return to her cabbages and turkeys at Peckham, she had almost gone distracted: that residence appeared a thousand times more dreadful to her, since she had been initiated into the amusements of London'. Nothing could console her but the promise of Miss Hamilton and her friends to come and spend the following season at Hextal while the Court were to be at Tunbridge Wells, and nothing but the anticipation of this remained to keep her from falling back into her previous state of despondency.

The Court duly set out for the Wells, and the Chevalier de Gramont, Miss Hamilton, and George repaired to Hextal to visit Elizabeth Whetenhall and drive out to the informal gaieties which were taking place some ten miles distant from her home. They were presently invited by Lady Muskerry to attend the party at Somerhill. It may have been there that the scene of 'A Peckham Frolic' was set, and it may also have been Elizabeth Whetenhall, playing 'Cinderella' in her romantic little adventure, who provided the *motif* for the play.

The unfortunate lady soon afterwards returned as a dutiful wife to her unhappy environment. It seems to have been more than she was able to endure, for she died childless in 1664 and was buried in Peckham Church. Her epitaph, duly appended by a mourning but inconsiderate husband, reads as follows:

'Here lye the remaines of Elizabeth Whetenhal second wife of Thomas Whetenhal of this parish ESQ-: eldest daughter of Henry Bedingfield of Beckhal in the County of Norfolk ESQ-: and grandchild to Edward Paston of the same place and county, here interred by her who having faithfully and exemplarily discharged the part of an affectionate wife, dutiful child, sincere friend and which comprehends all of a good Christian, after she had been married XI years VII months without issue departed on Ye 24th daye of February 1664 in the 27th yeare of her age leavinge, withall for her untimely, though as to herself most mature and happy end, a generale sadnesse, but with her husband so particular a resentment as he could rather wish engrave on his owne than her monumente: Requiescat in Pace—Amen.'

The family continued to live at Peckham into the eighteenth century, and there were among the Twysden archives in the Muniment Room at Roydon deeds relating to a mortgage raised on Peckham Place and its appurtenances in 1698 by Thomas and Henry Whetenhall for £1,200, to which contract Sir Henry Bedingfield is also a party.[1] There are many other documents referring to contracts for sale of lands in East Peckham by the Whetenhalls to the Twysdens in the early part of the eighteenth century, including the estate of Court Lodge in 1715 for £2,545.[2]

About 1860 a curious discovery was made in Peckham Church when, during the incumbency of Mr. Onslow,[3] the old pews were being removed and replaced. Under the old pew occupied by generations of the Whetenhall family an urn was excavated, containing the remains of a heart which was presumed to belong to a female member of the family. As the last of the Whetenhalls alienated Peckham Place to the Earl of Westmorland, who died in 1762, the relic must have been preserved for well over a hundred years.

[1] Lot 224 in Messrs. Sotheby Wilkinson's catalogue of the sale, April 1892.
[2] Lot 112, ditto.   [3] List of Incumbents, p. 32.

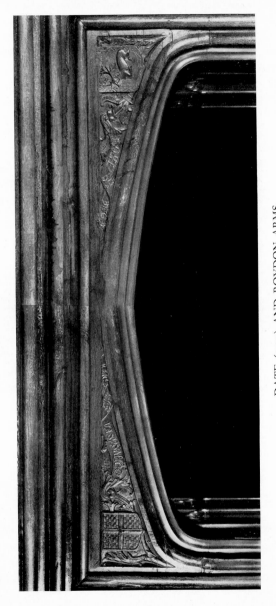

DATE (1535) AND ROYDON ARMS

Motto and Crest in Spandrels over the Porch leading to inner courtyard

Early in the reign of Henry VIII there came to Peckham one Thomas Roydon, possessed of wealth, upon whom fame and fortune had smiled at an early age. He was the son of Thomas Roydon of Ramsey in Essex by his second wife and was born in 1484. The Roydons were descended from the Robert de Reydon of Reydon in Suffolk in the time of Henry II. History does not relate how Thomas the founder of Roydon in Kent was blest by fortune so young, but there can be no doubt about the substantial nature of his inheritance when it is seen how widely and rapidly he acquired estates in that county during the early years of his residence there, and raised the mansion in which he finally settled down with his wife and family.

About 1509 Thomas married Margaret, daughter of William Whetenhall of Hextal, her father being as we have seen a man of good position and considerable property. He was the ancestor of George and Thomas Whetenhall, who in turn subsequently became lords of the manor of East Peckham. Margaret's dowry on her marriage consisted of the manor of Gore in Tunstall, near Sittingbourne, together with lands in that part, and it is probable that it was there that she and her husband spent the first few years of their married life and from whence they decided to acquire the manor or tenement of 'Fortune' (happily named) in East Peckham, very close to Margaret's old home.

The motto of Thomas Roydon—'*Come je Trowe*' (*Trouve*) —is to be found in one of the spandrils of the arch leading from the porch into the hall at Roydon, and if anything so ingenuous and straightforward may be paraphrased, it might perhaps be rendered 'I take anything that comes'. At any rate it is remarkably apt for a man who knew his own mind and how to set about living usefully. He was connected with the Nevills of Birling by the marriage of his eldest son George, and it appears he sent ninety-one men to Lord Burgavenny's[1] (George Nevill's) muster at

---

[1] Alternative spelling 'Bergavenny'.

Canterbury in 1522, and went surety in the sum of two hundred pounds for that gentleman when he was fined 10,000 marks on one occasion. He was also a trustee of his will.

Thomas was a Commissioner of the Peace from 1531 till he died, and was one of the gentlemen of Kent appointed to attend on the King's own person at the time of the Northern Rebellion in 1536, when he brought with him twenty men. At the landing of Anne of Cleves at Dover in 1539, on the occasion of the King's fourth marriage, he was commanded to attend the Duke of Suffolk with his retainers, and in 1544 was present at the departure of an expedition to France with six of his men. It is also recorded that Thomas Roydon of Gt. Peckham, Esquire, contributed in 1542 twenty marks by way of a loan to the King.[1]

On the opposite spandril of the arch referred to are the words *Domus ista fuit edita 1535*, and this is taken as the authority for the date when the house was built. There are carved above also the arms of Roydon and a Buck Lodged (probably the crest), and this appears carved elsewhere in the house together with the motto *Comme je Trouve*.

There has been some controversy as to what Fortune consisted of when the Roydons first acquired it. Although it is proposed to discuss the architecture and evolution of the house in a later chapter, it is necessary at this stage to form some impression of what may have been there at the time that we are considering. From the East Peckham deeds and inquisitions after the death of Thomas Roydon, the place does not appear to have been attached to any large estate. The Hextal and Westmorland estates lay to the south and west respectively, and to the east was the manor of Lomewood (or Bromes), which together with Fortune in the year 1500 'were held of Richard Fane in socage by Fealty and Rent and were worth £20 a year'. Fortune must be assumed therefore to have been a small holding of its own at this time.

[1] *Arch. Cant.*, vol. xi, p. 401.

Hasted says:

'In East or Great Peckham, there is an eminent seat called Roydon Hall, which was before called Fortune, but was of no great account until about the beginning of Henry VIII, when Roydon of Suffolk came into this county and seated himself here and erected this pile upon which he fixed his own name. He was a descendant of Sir Robert de Reydon (or Roydon) of Suffolk, kt. Temp. K. Edward I whose grandson was one Rauf Roydon.'

There seems to be little doubt that Thomas Roydon acquired this small property and built the garden towers, walls, and gateway to surround the demesne upon which his mansion was about to be built and it was afterwards that he enlarged the estate. The time when it was considered safe to dispense with substantial protection had not yet arrived, as will be seen in a later chapter. Nor can we reconcile the fact that such massive walls were erected to surround a small farm-house which, if we are to believe the early county historians, Fortune was before Thomas Roydon came there.

Thomas and Margaret had seven children, two sons and five daughters, and if it had not been for a fortunate occurrence, the history of Roydon and its families would have turned out very differently.

Ill luck pursued both sons;[1] the elder, George, after making a good marriage with Katherine Nevill of the distinguished family at Birling and having one son, was convicted of being an accomplice in the murder of a keeper of Lord Dacre while unlawfully hunting deer in his park at Pelhams in Sussex. He was executed in 1546 and his son Thomas, disinherited by his father's felony, died at an early age without issue. The second son, William, married Joan, daughter of Thomas Wilford[2] of Cranbrook in 1544 and had a son Thomas (called the younger), but by 1548 William was dead. His son in 1557,

---

[1] According to Streatfeild, 'One if not both the sons of Thomas Roydon were drowned in the Medway near Brand Bridges.'

[2] 'Thomas Wilford had issue Joanna (or Joan), who married (1) William Roydon and on his death (2) John Sydenham. Thomas Wilford married secondly Rose, daughter of William Whetenhall' (Roydon Pedigree).

when his grandfather died, was found to be heir to all his property, but being only 12 years old he became a ward of the Crown. Under this yoke he appears to have chafed, for in the next year he married one Eleanor Verney 'without the Queen's Licence having been obtained' and thereby became liable to a fine of £200, no small sum in those days. This unpropitious event, together with the fact that no children resulted from the marriage, was followed soon after in 1565 by his untimely death. Thus the male line failed entirely and the inheritance fell to be divided among the five daughters and co-heirs. It was the energy and sagacity of the third daughter Elizabeth (born in 1523), by then Lady Golding, which saved Roydon and averted the partition of the estates. She arranged by quitclaims and fines to purchase the interest of her four sisters and persuaded their husbands to agree. This appears to have been done amicably, and Elizabeth thus preserved her father's valuable and extensive property and manors and obtained the release for ever from all claims against her title.

Of the other daughters Margaret the eldest married Hugh Catlin of West Malling in 1565, by whom she had children, and secondly Everard Digby, about whom nothing is known. Anne married Henry De la Haye, by whom she had one son Nevill. Mary the fourth daughter married in 1541/2 as his second wife Thomas Darell of Scotney[1] in Lamberhurst and had one son Henry and four daughters. Alice, the youngest, who was 38 in 1565, married William Heron of Addiscombe and secondly Oliver St. John of Lambeth and of the county of Wiltshire, but does not appear to have had any surviving children of her own. By 1565, however, Elizabeth aged 42 had married her third husband, and to her shall be devoted a full account in a later chapter.

Thomas Roydon died in 1557, and by the inquisitions taken at Rochester in the same year after his death he is

---

[1] Genealogical Tree of the Darells of Scotney showing the connexion of the Roydons with that family, through Alice Whetenhall and Mary Roydon: *Arch. Cant.*, vol. xvii, p. 47.

shown to have possessed, at some time or other before making over properties to his daughters and sons-in-law, four manors:

The Manor of Gore in Tunstall, made over to his son William and Joan his wife on their marriage in 1544/5.

The Manor of Ringes in Wouldham and St. Margarets, also made over to William and Joan on their marriage.

The Manor of Hall Place in East Barmynge devised to his son George and his wife Katherine on their marriage in 1536. This reverted in 1541, when he predeceased his father.

The Manor of Lomewood or Bromes in East Peckham with which was incorporated Fortune. This property remained the original Roydon property and appertains to this day.

Besides these he had lands in the parishes of Nettlested, Wateringbury, Mereworth, Hadlow, Birling, Aylesford, Burham, St. Margarets, Wouldham, Boxley, Barming, Tunstall, Milton, Sittingbourne, Doddington, Newman, and Middleton in the county of Kent.

Thomas Roydon was one of those who 'Procured his landes in ye county of Kent to be disgavelled'[1] by the Act of Parliament passed in that year for the purpose . . . in the 31st year of the reign of King Henry VIII (1539).

[1] i.e. rendered free of the imposition of Gavelkind.

'Gavelkind' (*Ency. Brit.*): A peculiar system of tenure, associated chiefly with the county of Kent, but found also in other parts of England. In Kent all land was presumed to be holden by this tenure until the contrary was proved, but some lands have been *disgavelled* by particular statutes.

It is more correctly described as 'Socage Tenure', subject to the custom of Gavelkind. The chief peculiarities of the custom were:

(1) A tenant could alienate his lands by feoffment at 15 years of age.

(2) There was no escheat on attainder for felony.

(3) Generally the tenant could dispose of his lands by will.

(4) In intestacy the estate descended to the sons (or in the case of deceased sons to their representatives) in equal shares—'Every son is as great a gentleman as the eldest son is'. Though females claiming in their own right were postponed to males, yet by representation they inherited together with them.

(5) A wife was dowable of one-half instead of one-third of the land.

(6) A widower might be tenant by courtesy of half, without having had any issue, but only so long as he remained unmarried.

Gavelkind, was, previous to the Conquest, the general custom of the realm, but was then succeeded by the Feudal Law of Primogeniture. It was abolished by the Law of Property Act, 1922, and the Administration of Estates Act, 1925.

Dame Margaret Roydon died many years after him in 1576, up to which time she enjoyed the manor 'by right of increase'. They were both buried in the church of East Peckham, which overlooks Roydon and its lands. Fortune we hear of no more. It has now become definitely of some account, although the old name died out and the place became 'Roydon's Place' which lapsed into Roydon, the name it has borne ever since. We shall now trace the affairs of the next generation and show how the estate through its heiress and benefactress passed by marriage to the Twysdens, continuing from a long descent elsewhere in the county, the second family that became great at Roydon and directed its fortunes through good times and ill for the next 250 years.

Piety, a high devotion to duty, and an ever-present desire to improve the lot of their dependants and those in the small community of which they were the head, may have been the aim and incentive of the Tudor squire and his lady, such a worthy couple as were typically personified in Thomas and Margaret Roydon.

The following is an abstract of the Will of Thomas Roydon:

'In the name of God Amen, the 10th. day of August 1557. I Thomas Roydon of East Peckham, County Kent, Esquire, do order and make this my testament and last Will.

'My body to be buried in the Church of East Peckham. I will that my Executors shall bestow on the day of my burial to the poor of East Peckham 20/-. Also I bequeath to the Vicar of East Peckham for my tithes negligently omitted 2/-. I bequeath to the Parish Church of East Peckham a suit of vestments of crimson velvet.

'Also I will that Margaret Roydon, my wife, shall have the custody of such things as I hereafter have bequeathed to Thomas Roydon, my grandson, during her natural life. I will that Thomas Roydon my grandson have my "seled" bed with curtains, covering and all other (things) as it stands in the great chamber over the great parlour, and also all my gold and rings. I bequeath to George Cattelenn (Catlin) my gown of taffeta. I bequeath to John

Sydnam,[1] brother to Thomas Roydon my grandson 20/- yearly. I make Margaret Roydon my wife, George Clarke, Esquire "Hew" Catlin, Esquire, George Molton, Gent, and William Iden, Gent, executors of this my last will and testament.

'This is the last Will of me the said Thomas Roydon. I will that all those lands whereof I am seised in fee simple in East Peckham and Netlestede or elsewhere in the county of Kent shall be in the disposition of my executors by the space of eight years after my decease and at the end of the said term I will that my executors account for the residue to the said Thomas. Further I devise to the said Thomas all the lands to have and to hold after the said term to the said Thomas and his heirs of his body lawfully begotten, and for lack of such issue to Margaret Catlin, Ann Delahey, Marie (Elizabeth) Vaughan, Elizabeth (Mary) Darrell and Alice Heron my daughters, and to the heirs of their bodies lawfully begotten, and for lack of such issue to *John Sydnam* brother to Thomas Roydon my grandson and his heirs for ever.

'I devise to Nicholas Webb and Clemancie his wife my tenement at Prickles Hill in East Peckham during their lives and the life of the longest liver of them.

'Proved March 9th. 1559 by the oath of George Catlin proctor of Margaret, relict and executrix named in the said Will.'

The Will of Margaret Roydon his wife, daughter of William Whetenhall, who survived him many years and was buried at East Peckham on June 23rd, 1576, is as follows:

'This is the last will and testament of me Margaret Roydon made the 19th. January 18 Q Elizabeth (1575–6).

'To my daughter's son Roger Twiesden 40/- to buy him a ring. To my daughter's daughter Margaret Deringe 40/- to buy her a ring. The residue of my goods I bequeath to my daughter Goldinge whom I make sole executrix.

'Debts owing to me—My daughter's son George Catlyn £40. Proved 2nd. August 1576 by Edward Bigge proctor of Dame Elizabeth Goldinge, Executrix. . . .

[1] William, second son of Thomas Roydon the elder, married in Jan. 1544/5 Joan Wilford, daughter of Thomas Wilford of Cranbrook. He died in 1548, but left a son Thomas Roydon the younger, who in 1557 on the death of his grandfather was found to be heir to the whole of his estate. William's widow (Joan) married John Sydenham and had another son John, who thus was a step-brother of Thomas Roydon the younger.

CHAPTER IV

THE MANOR

AMONG the records of the county of Kent there is no
mention of a Manor of Roydon; but the house is
essentially a manor-house and was erected as the seat
of a lord of several small manors lying around it, which
existed before Thomas Roydon built his residence on the
site of the little manor-house called 'Fortune'. It may not
be out of place, therefore, to examine the nature of a
manor-house and to describe some of the manorial customs and the functions of the lord of the manor himself.
Mr. Ditchfield, in his book *The Manor Houses of England*,
quotes a definition from Mr. Scargill-Bird's *Guide to the
Public Records* in which he describes a manor as 'a certain
circuit of ground granted by the King to some baron or
man of worth as an inheritance for him and his heirs
with the exercise of such jurisdiction within the said compass as the King saw fit to grant, and subject to the per-
formance of such services and yearly rents as were by the
grant required'.

The manor boundaries did not necessarily coincide with
those of the parish. A village might be divided into
several manors. There were often sub-grants made by a
rich lord to a lesser personage, and this procedure was
common until the reign of Edward I, after whose time no
new manors were created. The Norman chiefs holding
land direct of the King were called tenants-in-chief. They
in turn would sometimes make over a part to others,
called sub-tenants, who helped to provide the personnel
demanded by the King as his due to call upon in time of
need. In those days there were only about 1,400 people
who held land directly of the King.

A manor consisted of strips of land granted in portions
according to the substance of the tenant. A freeman had
'Lots' for the members of his family, and such names as

'Shots' and 'Furlongs' denoted measurements of land thus subdivided among the lesser people of the manor.

The manorial system had its beginning in Celtic and Saxon Britain, and was so deeply rooted in the soil that when the Romans came they were wise enough in their experience as colonists not to attempt the redistribution of the old shires and hundreds but to retain them in their original form with their village communities and re-organize them under Roman governors-general. The Roman lords and their country villas also played an important part in creating centres around which clustered these settlements. Towns were relatively scarce and a great distance apart, so that not more than a small proportion of the surrounding country dwellers could gain access to their fortified walls in order to avoid destruction at the hands of the plundering bodies of wild men from the north and west who descended upon them from time to time. Towns were centres for disposing of government and for dispensing justice throughout the various provinces under the Roman régime. Hence these small communities or manors outside the towns came into existence primarily for the purpose of mutual aid and self-protection. When William the Norman came hundreds of years afterwards he found in Saxon England the elements of a feudal system which had continued to develop in spite of the successive invasions of Norseman and Dane. The feudal system is usually represented as a sweeping and fundamental change brought about by William the Conqueror, but in reality it was little more than a gradual development receiving the stimulus of the fresh and active Norman administration.

The tillers of the soil dwelt in their small villages and worked for themselves in the forest clearings and uplands under the lord of the manor, who gave them protection and claimed from them in return a portion—either from the proceeds of their labour or by the periodical exaction of direct service to himself.

Those who rendered tribute in the form of service

E

derived the benefit, upon occasions, of a suit of clothes, which gradually developed into the 'uniform', the outward sign of this service, and became the 'livery' of the great gentlemen of later days. The tribute levied in kind involved the offer of the best beast or fowl by the tenants to the lord of the manor, and for this custom we have to be grateful, in that it was the foundation of stock-breeding in the highly specialized form for which England more lately became famous. The finest specimens were thus selected and reared under the best breeding conditions inside the manor demesne, where the greatest care and the most expert knowledge would be likely to exist, in addition to the warmest stables and barns.

As an insurance against times of common danger all gave their allegiance and were in return given the right of protection inside the manor walls.

The manor-house was the demesne and usually the residence of the lord of the manor, and was situated as a rule in the middle of the village—near the church and the rectory.

The manor lord was looked up to and respected by his little community, and though his authority was by no means absolute he was so far trusted as to have become the recognized arbiter in any quarrels affecting the rights of his tenants *inter se*, and thereby came to have from the earliest times the function of official judge in any local dispute that arose. The direct descendants of this office are, of course, the Justices of the Peace. Over a period of centuries the lord of the manor acquired rights which even in our own times have come into conflict with the authorities which have superseded the manor. As Mr. Hone, reviewing these matters from the standpoint of the development of local government during the last century, says:

'Parish and District Councils, in questions constantly arising touching village greens, recreation grounds, commons and rights of way, find that they have to reckon with him, (The Lord of the Manor), in the exercise of their newly acquired powers, and have to adjust their claims in accordance with the old Manorial rights enjoyed by him and his predecessors for centuries.'[1]

In the last decade the enfranchisement for a trifling and nominal consideration has proceeded apace and very soon the ancient dues will have become extinct.

News travelled no faster than the fastest horse, except when the alarm was signalled in cases of extreme danger by the lighting of beacons on high ground. On such occasions there would have been little chance of safety, without the protection of the manor, for these helpless little colonies of loyal but peace-loving Saxon retainers with their well-fed cattle and the crops harvested in their barns. Stock would have been constantly plundered and burned and cattle driven away if it had not been for the manor and its function of providing security for them.

We may imagine the consternation that reigned when the look-out reported the distant beacon ablaze and sounded the alarm by ringing the great bell. The gates would be hurriedly thrown open to admit villagers and tenants and their families and such belongings as they could gather up. All available shelter in the outhouses and barns would be made use of and all able-bodied men summoned to their respective stations at the walls, while the beacons illuminated the surrounding scene of activity and spread their message.

The alarm might prove serious or otherwise, but anything in the nature of an ordinary attack would be repulsed with ease and the plunderers would deem discretion the better part of valour and content themselves by making off with the few spoils they could collect outside the walls and disappear before the nearest garrison could turn out to inflict on them proper punishment. Few could afford to be outside the circle of the manorial protection which afforded temporary shelter within its precincts for all the dependants of the manor until danger was over— shelter for women and children and such belongings as

[1] *The Manor and Manorial Records*, by N. J. Hone.

could hastily be gathered together and such cattle as could be rounded up in time. The walls had to be manned and the lord of the manor would see to it that the periodical training was exacted from his subjects to ensure the defence being effective. How simple and self-sufficient was this primitive form of existence—protection in return for services in time of danger; food, clothing, and wages for labour in times of peace! As long as the lord of the manor could adequately defend his walls—and against the usual attacks of light-armed marauders this was not difficult— little harm was suffered by the occasional destruction of crops or the rough dwellings in which his people lived. At worst it was only a temporary setback.

Thus reigned the lord of the manor, for the most part in undisturbed and uneventful peace—the executor of local justice, the representative of his shire or hundred, and the administrator of the manorial estates which usually endowed him with moderate wealth and prosperity. Most of this wealth was invariably put back into the land and went to improving the lot of his people. In war-time or upon state occasions the royal grant under which he held the manor required him to send a number of men under arms, according to the size of his estates, to defend the shores or form part of an expeditionary force in the event of war abroad.

The *Manor-Houses* that still survive and with which England is richly endowed may be divided roughly into three periods: the pre-Tudor, before the middle of the fifteenth century; the Tudor, from about 1450 to 1550; and the Elizabethan, from the latter date until the end of James I's reign. In dealing with the plan and development of the manor-house we must first briefly survey the effect of the English Renaissance upon the architecture of those periods during which nearly all our manor-houses were erected.

Although the scope of our subject does not pretend to include the earlier castles nor the magnificent palaces of the later era, we shall find there are certain factors in common to all three, and an interwoven thread of progressive development running through them. We will accordingly deal with them in the order of the loosely defined periods referred to above.

Until the end of the fifteenth century an Englishman's home was his castle, not only in name but in fact. The great castles and the lesser defended dwellings were constructed for security and, as was frequently necessary in those times, for resistance. The standing and wealth of the owner were displayed in this outward and visible sign of strength, but not for this purpose alone. The ingenuity of protective devices might at any moment be put to the practical test.

The methods employed were numerous and are to be found more or less in common throughout England. The surrounding walls were of great thickness and considerable height, being covered at every angle from battlements and lancet windows in the main building. The outer circle of defence was a moat, if it was practicable, and a site was often chosen to admit of the construction of this feature. The approaches across it were strongly guarded and covered by the keep. At corners or intervals of the main building were towers or bastions of great strength and commanding height. Good instances showing all these features are Bodiam, Hurstmonceaux, Allington, and Leeds Castle. In active defence they were manned by bowmen, light-armed slingers, and javelin-throwers, with bodies of men in reserve collected above every possible vantage-point which might be gained by a massed attack, to tip over boulders and boiling pitch upon any who might have succeeded in approaching near enough to attempt the scaling of the walls.

The lesser demesnes relied more upon their outer defences than the actual fortification of the house itself. Great Chalfield in Wiltshire, dating from the latter part of Henry VI's reign, is a fair example of a manor-house built with little in the way of defence long before the time when it was considered safe to be without it; but the precautions were by no means disregarded, reliance being placed upon the sighting of the house and the cleverly situated moat lying to the north-east.

Invariably we find that the Englishman's home was evolved according to his needs. In times of disturbance the first need was very naturally safety and protection, while in times of peace, development was dictated by the desire for greater comfort and adornment. As England emerged from the Wars of the Roses into the era of calm and reconstruction introduced by Henry VII the elaborate precautions for defence were gradually dispensed with. Building for peaceful occupation and enjoyment began to progress very rapidly, and the Tudor period was the result of this activity. The castle keep gave way to the gatehouse, and that in turn a century later had become a gateway which it was the custom to make an architectural feature by giving it much dignity and ornamentation to make up for its loss of usefulness. The old defensive walls became lower until, in Elizabethan times, their breast-height only served the purpose of marking the formality of courtyard or garden. Battlements were suc-ceeded by plain-pointed gables, and although stepped gables were frequently introduced, it was mainly for decoration or distinction, to give the added importance which the fastidious Elizabethan era demanded. Every rich man of the time desired to build a mansion that would exceed in beauty and size that of his friend or political rival. The excellence of his dwelling was expressed in the elaboration of its design and the luxury of its adornment, for it must be remembered that most Tudor and many Elizabethan squires were their own architects.

But to return to the sequence, let us examine the layout of a Tudor house. A sketch of the Manor is included, and while no such place exists, we have endeavoured to illustrate, for example, most of the usual features em-ployed in fortification and at the same time to give an idea of the general ground-plan of a typical, but moderate-sized, demesne of early Tudor times. A rough road led

[Copyright]

ROYDON IN 1860
from an etching by M. W. HYDE

up to the gatehouse from which a drive, used on formal occasions, approached the entrance to the courtyard. Inside this, usually (but not always) immediately opposite to it, lay the main door of the house giving access through the 'screens' into the hall. This was the official chamber for all gatherings and motes, on which occasions the lord of the manor held the court, attended by his bailiff. It was the duty of the bailiff to keep the Court Rolls and record therein the necessary entries relating to tithe, rent, and other dues by the tenants of the estate. At Martinmas, November 11th, he levied his annual heriot, or the right of claiming the best head of cattle from his freemen of the manor and other less burdensome kind, such as pig or fowl, from his villeins, cottars, and serfs.

The great chamber was in more senses than one the focal point. It had an open-timbered roof, the full height of the house, and therefore effectively severed it into two parts, and divided the upper floors also, so that to reach one end of the house from the other it was necessary to pass through the hall. The rest of the house naturally came to be built around it, according to needs and customs. Opening out of one end of the hall was the parlour, and next to it the lord's room or 'solar', close to which was the muniment room—the storeroom for all records and valuables. The community were privileged to hand over their treasures for safe keeping, together with those belonging to the owner of the house. At the opposite end of the hall from the living apartments were the kitchens and domestic offices. They were reached by the 'screens' before mentioned, an important feature of the Tudor house which served the double purpose of shutting off the serving-rooms from the hall and preventing those within being exposed to the view of any one entering the outer door. In the centre of the hall was the long table which accommodated all the household and retainers at meals. At right angles to it, upon a dais 'above the salt', was a table at which the lord sat with his family. There was usually a bay window towards the end nearest the dais, and opposite it, in the inner wall, a large fire-place which served to warm the whole chamber. If there was a gallery it was at the end farthest from the dais, over the screens. The whole arrangement is easily seen among many of the college halls. The domestic offices usually consisted of a pantry, buttery, and larder, with cellars beneath, and the larger houses were also provided, in addition, with bakery, brewery, and laundry. In the lesser houses those essentials, for which there was not room in the house-plan, were accommodated in adjacent out-houses.

Around the house were barns and granaries, cattle-sheds, piggeries, forge, stables, and equipage. Commanding these were the protecting walls, towers, and gatehouse in which the watchmen and guard had their quarters.

There was considerable evolution and variation of this general plan in the Elizabethan era, but the essential features of it were maintained even in the great palaces, such as Kirby, Sutton, Nonsuch, and many others. At about this time greater refinement in custom became fashionable and the hall tended to become smaller in proportion to the size of the house. More state apartments were introduced, and guests and retainers ceased to dine together. The magnificence of the dwelling came to lie rather in the number and ornamentation of its apartments than in the spaciousness of any particular one, although this by no means entailed the abandonment of any essential feature. The hall retained its place of importance far into the Elizabethan period, by which time the wealth of the great courtiers and gentlemen had so far increased, owing to freedom from war and discoveries of great riches abroad, that it became the fashion to embody, both within and without, some of the luxurious effects studied by the Renaissance masters on the Continent. Henry VIII and Wolsey had introduced the influence of the Italian Renaissance into English architecture as early as 1520, and although little trace of the names of foreign masters can be found, the importance of the fact lay in their influence in turn upon our own master-workmen. It appears to have been mainly through lack of money that this influence did not more rapidly permeate the character of the dwellings of lesser importance. In all probability the King was employing most of the skilled foreigners himself in the building of colleges and palaces. It is, however, interesting to note that while Oxburgh (1482) is pure English-Gothic with no trace of the Italian motive, Layer Marney, only twenty years later, and Hengrave (1538) show definite signs of it. Many other and possibly better examples could be quoted. One other point must be especially emphasized in regard to the Tudor period as distinct from the Elizabethan. It is the lack of symmetry in the plans and elevations. Therein lies much of the charm and beauty, which is by no means haphazard, in the workmanship and artistic instinct of the English master-builders of these early times. Let us take Compton Wynyates as an example of this. There is no attempt at symmetry, though there is a pleasing balance in the architecture, while the effect of the grouping is most interesting in the structure as a whole. Upon the invasion of the Italian and later the German and Dutch styles, symmetry became almost the first consideration in exterior effect. The latter half of the sixteenth century showed a quickening in the evolution of the English country mansion and house, unprecedented up till that time. To this period, the Elizabethan proper, belong Kirby and Montacute, and their embellishments are a good example of the unstinted extravagance that was lavished upon external, as well as internal, decoration. Even the smaller country houses were rarely without some feature to express the importance of being fashionable. The entrance porch at Roydon is an unpretentious example of the owner's desire to introduce a suggestion of the Italian Renaissance. Viewed from within the frame of the courtyard arch the ornament is simple and effective and harmonizes well with the architecture of what had originally been a plain and somewhat austere front.

We have devoted a separate chapter to the architecture of Roydon and have dealt at length with the gradual stages of its development from the time of building. Generally speaking, the ground-plan has suffered little if any structural change since the foundations were laid and none of the external walls has been altered in outline. It is therefore possible to trace the resemblance in Roydon to a typical manor-house of the Tudor period, such as we have endeavoured to describe.

CHAPTER V

ELIZABETH ROYDON

WE have already seen what an important part Elizabeth, the third daughter of Thomas Roydon,
played in saving Roydon and its estates, by her
wisdom and foresight, from being divided and appor-
tioned among her sisters and co-heirs under her father's
will. Whichever of them had inherited the demesne itself
for her portion would probably have had insufficient
money to support it without the revenues of the surrounding manors, and there can be little doubt that a generation
or two would have witnessed Roydon's demise.

At Bradbourne there is a fine portrait of her dated 1587
when sixty-four years of age, and this portrait must have
hung at Roydon till the beginning of the nineteenth century together with those of many other of her Twysden
descendants, preserved by their late owner, Sir John
Twisden[1] of Bradbourne. In the left-hand upper corner
of the picture there is a grim-looking skull set into a niche,
beneath which is her epitaph *Pietas honoratior annis*, which
appears to have been painted in at a later date after her
death.

Elizabeth was fortunate and wise in the choice of her
first husband, and it is the children of this marriage whose
careers we are concerned in following. By her subsequent
husbands she had no children. She was only 18 when she
married William Twysden of Chelmington, a manor lying

[1] Sir John Ramskill Twisden, 12th and last baronet of Bradbourne, died Nov.
7, 1937, aged 80. He left his family papers to the Kent Archaeological Society,
and certain family portraits to the National Portrait Gallery and the Kent
Archaeological Society.
The different spelling of the name may be observed. The Twysdens of
Roydon have stuck religiously to the *y*, whereas it is noticeable that the Bradbourne branch adopted an alternative form of spelling, using the *i*, as also did
Lady Cholmley previous to her marriage. It may have been a matter of courtesy,
by mutual consent, that the 'Twysden' spelling should be retained by the Roydon
branch (which held the older Baronetcy), and not used by other branches thereafter, to distinguish them.

ELIZABETH ROYDON
afterwards Lady Golding

two miles south-west of Ashford in the parish of Great Chart near Wye.

The Twysdens were of Kent, and traced their ancestry back to the time of Edward I, in the second year of whose reign Adam de Twysden, according to Hasted, was residing at the 'Den' or borough of Twysden in the parish of Sandhurst, Kent. Charles Seymour, however, in *A New Survey of Kent* (1776), differs from Hasted's account and tells us that the family took their name from the Manor of Twisden near Goudhurst, some ten miles from Sandhurst, where they were living in the twenty-first year of that reign. Both Adam and his next brother Gregory died without issue, leaving the succession to be carried on by the youngest brother John.[1] His descendant Roger in the reign of Henry V married Elizabeth, daughter and heiress of Thomas Chelmington esquire of Chelmington, and in her right became possessed of this manor. Their eldest son, Roger Twysden of Wye, married Jane Sharp (*née* Cooper) and by her had two sons, the elder of whom, William, married in 1541 Elizabeth Roydon and thus became possessed of Roydon through his wife's inheritance. It is a curious coincidence that two properties came to the early Twysdens by their marriages to two heiresses both named Elizabeth.

Chelmington Manor remained in the family until Sir Thomas Twysden in the reign of Queen Anne alienated it to a Mr. Hooker, and beyond that we need not trace it.

William and Elizabeth left Chelmington soon after their marriage, and went to live at Roydon with her father. It is recorded that in the second year of King Edward VI 'William Twisenden', as he was then written, 'procured his lands to be dis-gavelled[2] by Act of Parliament'. It must be assumed that the Roydon succession, owing to the failure of the sons and the disinheritance of the grandson, was decided at about this time[3] and, by the influence of the astute Elizabeth, no doubt made over to her husband

---

[1] Pedigree, p. 62.   [2] Note, p. 45.
[3] Thomas Roydon did not die until 1557.

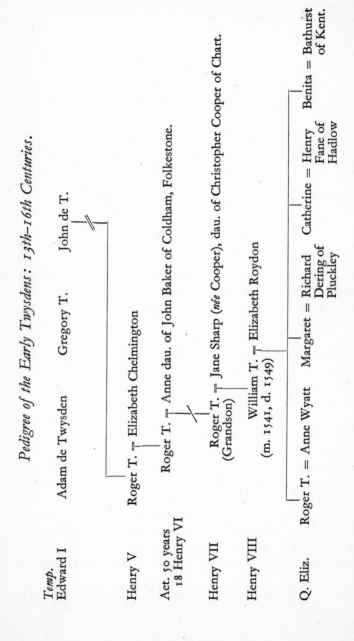

Pedigree of the Early Twysdens: 13th–16th Centuries.

Temp.
Edward I   Adam de Twysden   Gregory T.   John de T.

Henry V   Roger T. = Elizabeth Chelmington

Act. 50 years
18 Henry VI   Roger T. = Anne dau. of John Baker of Coldham, Folkestone.

Henry VII   Roger T. = Jane Sharp (née Cooper), dau. of Christopher Cooper of Chart.
(Grandson)

Henry VIII   William T. = Elizabeth Roydon
(m. 1541, d. 1549)

Q. Eliz.   Roger T. = Anne Wyatt   Margaret = Richard Dering of Pluckley   Catherine = Henry Fane of Hadlow   Benita = Bathurst of Kent.

for their children. It is the only son Roger, born in 1542, in whom we are mainly interested for the purpose of this story. There were three daughters: the eldest, Margaret, married Richard Dering of Pluckley, but of the two youngest, Catherine and Bennet, there is no reliable information. It is believed they both died young and, although married, without issue. Little is known of William Twysden. The marriage only lasted eight years, and he died in 1549.

His younger brother, Thomas Twysden of Wye, became a Benedictine Monk of the Great Abbey of Battle, which in those days was a foundation offering a worthy retreat to the younger members of even the greatest families. The Great Abbey *de Bello* presented not only the advantage of a near neighbourhood but also of a close connexion with the town of Wye, where was his own home, the Manor of Chelmington being among the earliest properties acquired by the great Norman monastery itself. Although Thomas does not appear to have attained higher rank than the order of deacon, he would no doubt have progressed further had not the long-threatened blow fallen upon the monastic system in England. Significant warning was given by the suppression first of the alien and then of the lesser priories, and finally even the great Abbey *De Bello* fell by the order of the Reformation to the *Spolia Opima* of Henry VIII's Augmentation Office. Amongst the documents that used to be kept in the muniment room at Roydon, none was more interesting than that relating to the dispensation from his monastic vows granted by Cardinal Pole to Thomas 'Bede' (*alias* Twysden) and the confirmation of this order under the Great Seal of England by Henry VIII. This was copied word for word from the original probate at Roydon by Mr. Lambert Larking in 1834 and published by the Kent Archaeological Society.[1]

[1] *Arch. Cant.*, vol. viii, p. 61.

'Warrant from Reginald, Cardinal Pole, to his Vicar-General David Poole, to grant a Pardon to Thomas Twysden *alias* Bede, late a Monk of Battle Abbey, dissolved on his own Recantation and Petition, absolving him from the Sin of

As mentioned above, William Twysden of Chelmington died on November 26th, 1549, and the cardinal granted this dispensation to Bede allowing him, contrary to monastic custom and procedure, to become an executor of his brother's will. The order is dated 1556, seven years after the latter's death, and was necessary because the possession of property or the making of a will was a sin in the case of a monk and involved the confiscation of all such property and the peril of being denied Christian burial.

It is probable that William realized that there was every likelihood of his widow marrying again and he had no desire to prevent her from doing so. Nevertheless, he considered it prudent, in view of the fact that his son and heir was only 7 years old, to protect his estate during the boy's minority. The precaution as it turned out was a very wise one, and he may even have had some premonition that it might be necessary.

His brother Thomas may also have been the one person to whom he desired to entrust such a responsibility and he thus disposed it in his will. It is a high tribute to Thomas's loyalty and devotion to his family that he persevered in obtaining the dispensation.

Elizabeth's eldest son Roger lived at Roydon with his

secularising and obtaining goods and lands, licensing him to execute the office of Deacon, to remain as Secular, and to hold a Benefice until the regular places are restored; and also to retain his property on condition of his bequeathing it to the said Monastery or to Religious uses (*which he never did*) 18 Feb. 1556/7 with the Privy Seal of Cardinal Pole attached.

'License from Cardinal Pole to Thomas Twysden, Deacon in the Diocese of Canterbury, to act as the Executor to the will of his deceased brother William, in conjunction with Elizabeth widow and Executrix of the said William Twysden.

'Dispensation from Monastic Vows granted by Archbishop Thomas Cranmer to Bede with license to secularise and hold a Benefice with Cure of Souls— Lambeth 12 June 1538. Letters Patent under the Great Seal of Henry VIII confirming Bede's License—Westminster 12 June 1538.

'Letters Patent under the Great Seal of Henry VIII granting a pension of 10 Marks per an. to Thomas Bede, late a Monk of the Dissolved Abbey of Battle.' (No. 365 in Messrs. Sotheby's Sale Catalogue.)

Note. These highly interesting documents are important evidence of the course pursued on the ejection of the Monks, and the disreputable efforts of the Crown and the Legate to recover the property deemed otherwise lost to the Church.

mother, but did not succeed until her death in 1595, when he was 53 years old. He pursued a military career within the county, taking a prominent part in what, in more modern times, would have been the Yeomanry. In 1588 he was present with his contingent at Tilbury Camp, where he was in command of a troop of gentlemen-at-arms, forming part of the Queen's garrison to resist the landing of the Spaniards from the Armada. He was appointed by royal warrant to be captain of a troop of horse known as the Aylesford Light Horse in 1598, during which year he also became a sheriff of the county. He had married in 1565 Ann, daughter of Sir Thomas Wyatt[1] the younger, of Allington Castle, the illustrious leader of the Rebellion of 1553 which ended in his death on the scaffold.

But in Elizabeth's reign the Wyatts received back much of their lands and their prestige substantially recovered, no doubt in due recognition of their services and efforts on behalf of the Queen during the troublesome years that preceded her accession.

Elizabeth Twysden was a devout Protestant and took a profound interest in the affairs of the Church, as did every one of responsibility and position in those days of deep cleavage in religious matters. The proximity of her own domain to Maidstone, the centre of local government in the county, necessitated her periodical attendance there, and no doubt she was a frequent visitor to the home of her daughter-in-law, Allington Castle.[2] Here Tom Wyatt made his house a rendezvous for those of his more daring associates, and feelings ran high in the political and religious questions of the time. Mary was on the throne, mistrusted and misunderstood by her people. The most

---

[1] Note on the Wyatt family at end of this chapter.

[2] Allington was one of the seven great castles of Kent and formed part of the wide possessions of the Conqueror's half-brother Odo, Bishop of Bayeux. It was embattled by Royal Licence towards the end of the thirteenth century, and some of the original brickwork is still visible. Sir Henry Wyatt acquired the Castle in 1492 and opposed the pretensions of Richard III to the throne. He was imprisoned in the Tower where it was intended to starve him to death, but the story goes that he had a favourite cat who killed small birds and brought them to the bars of his prison chamber and thus saved his life. He was released and restored to favour by Henry VII and died at Allington in 1537.

misguided, yet the most single-minded, of the Tudors failed honestly to grasp the needs of Englishmen and to appreciate their fervent desire for unity in the Church by a wise and compromising moderation. She ignored those signs of the spirit of adventure, the growth of which her father and grandfather had fostered in their people. Mary could never visualize England as a principal state, but only as a pawn that needed to be linked up to a great sovereign power. Her guiding star was Spain, and her choice fell upon that ancient and bigoted empire, whose civilization already showed unmistakable signs of crumbling into decadence. Her narrow and solitary upbringing bred in her a fanatical leaning towards the Holy Roman Church in the extreme, and the passionate fervour with which she embraced the Catholic faith blinded her to any possibility of religious toleration or compromise in dealing with her subjects. Morbidly in her solitude, she framed her own and her country's future as one, dreaming of security for England under the patronage of Spain and of a marriage with the Spanish King to cement her kingdom and her faith.

Kent, as usual, was foremost in its opinions on these matters, and many Kentish lords and squires were gathering together to consider what action to take. Elizabeth Twysden was deeply interested in the comings and goings at Allington, and no doubt at one of these meetings met and fell in love with Cuthbert Vaughan, whom she married soon afterwards in 1551. He was 'a leading Protestant and prominent among the Reformers'. Through her romantic association with him, Elizabeth saw in her second husband a rising fame. His family were of Hargest, Herefordshire, on the borders of Wales. Young and handsome, full of Welsh enthusiasm, he was a man of energy and charm, already in the King's service. There is an engraving of his portrait in Drake's enlargement of Hasted's *Blackheath Hundred*, where a facsimile of his signature is also reproduced. By right of his manor of Honychild, granted to him by Edward VI, he was a lord of Romney

Marsh, which in those days called for considerable abili-
ties, both in matters respecting the administration of
valuable grazing-rights on his property and the duties that
brought him into close contact with the Cinque Ports and
their ever-increasing importance.

Elizabeth's career had hitherto pursued an even tenor.
She was still only 29 and in the prime of life when ambi-
tion drove her to take a part in the coming disruptions
and to plan a future for her new husband. Vaughan soon
provided her with more than enough excitement to satisfy
these aspirations. In 1553 he joined Wyatt's rising of the
men of Kent, and there is little doubt he was one of those
largely responsible for organizing the Rebellion and for
providing the money and support to enable it to be
launched with any prospect of success. The pretext was
ostensibly that of giving vent to indignation at the Queen's
favouritism towards her Catholic friends culminating in
the announcement of her intention to marry Philip of
Spain. If Mary had decided on her policy, and rightly
assessed her power to carry it out, she had certainly very
much misjudged the temper of her people. When Eng-
landers were adventuring everywhere abroad and meeting
Spaniards in opposition at every turn, this was no time to
make England Spain's vassal state, in flesh as in spirit, her
realm under the yoke of those tyrants of the Inquisition
and her religion under the domination of the Pope.
Wyatt's motives went further than inflaming his followers
against the existing order. It went beyond mere rebellion
as a form of protest and aimed at the capture of the Queen's
person with a view to placing the Princess Elizabeth on
the throne, thus to strike a blow for the Protestant cause
and at the same time to remove the influence of Renard
and all those much-hated Catholic ministers whom Mary
had chosen exclusively as her advisers.

At last all was prepared; the plans formulated behind
the austere walls of the castle were complete. The rebels
raised Wyatt's standard in Maidstone and marched forth
to win their supporters. The numbers increased like a

snowball, and approaching Rochester they were already many thousand strong. News of the insurrection reached the Queen in her council chamber at the Tower whither she had removed from her palace of Whitehall. The Duke of Norfolk was ordered to march and disperse the rebels immediately, and Captain Bret, with a thousand of the city's trained bands, was ordered out under the Duke's command. Wyatt had already reached Rochester and taken the castle when the royal troops arrived. Bret refused to fight his countrymen and deserting to Wyatt's standard, marched on with him to the Tower of London, where by this time the greatest consternation prevailed, and the hastiest preparation was being made of all the defences. The most unmoved was the Queen herself; she ordered resistance to the end, and relied upon her own strength of will in case she should be forced to make an appeal to the insurgents as a last resort. Amongst other things Wyatt demanded the immediate surrender of her person, and when all terms had been refused the storming of the Tower was begun. The story of this battle has been picturesquely described by Ainsworth and need not be told here, but the onslaught eventually failed, and Tom Wyatt and his leaders were captured. Wyatt himself, after great torture on the rack, died most bravely on the scaffold and protested to the last Princess Elizabeth's innocence of any knowledge of the plot. His estates in Aylesford and Maidstone were confiscated by the Crown, and his children forfeited their inheritance, until they were restored, as we have previously mentioned, in the following reign.[1]

One of the most enthusiastic suppressors of the rebellion was Sir Robert Southwell, Sheriff of Kent, and for his loyalty he was subsequently rewarded by large grants of land in Kent. He had been Master of the Rolls in the 35th year of King Henry VIII, when he obtained licence of alienation to sell his estates in Mereworth and else-

---

[1] Among the Twysden family portraits sold in October 1911 there was a picture of Sir Thomas Wyatt the younger.

where in Kent to Sir Edmund Walsingham, Lieutenant of the Tower of London, and Lady Anne Grey, his wife. Of these estates in Mereworth he had become possessed through marriage with Margaret, daughter and sole heir to Sir Thomas Nevill, Kt., of Yote's Court, fourth son of George, Lord Burgavenny,[1] who had bequeathed Yotes to this his younger son. Soon after Wyatt marched out of Allington Castle, Southwell took it over and imprisoned many of the ringleaders there and others in Maidstone Jail. He later set out with Lord Burgavenny and a small force from Malling to intercept Sir Henry Isley and the two Knevetts, who were marching from Sevenoaks to join Wyatt at Rochester. They effected their object by meeting and defeating the rebels in Wrotham upon Blacksole Field.[2]

Cuthbert Vaughan was, naturally, implicated in the rising, and was one of those arrested. As a friend of Nicholas Throckmorton, he had enlisted the latter's aid to influence the support of the merchants and well-to-do in the richer quarters of the city. The two-handled sword with which he had fought in the vanguard of an unsuccessful attack upon Whitehall became an heirloom which we shall allude to again in a later chapter. He was arrested and taken to the Tower on February 9th, where he was tried and pleaded guilty, but claimed his life through having been promised a pardon by a herald on the field. He was 'houselled' (i.e. communicated as a Catholic) on February 23rd and condemned to death on the 28th of that month in 1554. Being sent with others to be executed at Maidstone, he was, on March 12th, 'brought again out of Kent into the Tower by the importable suit of his wife'. Elizabeth, trying desperately to save her husband's life, prevailed through her influence in securing him another trial. A not very commendable idea occurred to him that he might obtain pardon for himself by helping to convict Throckmorton, so he decided to turn Queen's evidence against him. The jury, however, returned a verdict of

[1] See page 41. [2] *Arch. Cant.*, vol. iii.

'Not Guilty' against his popular and highly esteemed friend. Vaughan thus saved his own life, but it is not recorded how he extricated himself from the implications of the plot. The fact remains that he was again in the service of Queen Elizabeth in 1560 and this must be taken to show that he not only cleared himself, but secured for his past services in the royal cause some acknowledgement and reward; in the fifth year of her reign he was granted an addition to his estates in Romney Marsh by the Manor of Eastbridge, next to Honychild. The last that is heard of Vaughan is through a letter to his Sovereign expressing disappointment at the treatment meted out to him. He complained of neglect and asked permission to pass overseas 'to obtain the benefit of the Baths for his hurt'. He died soon afterwards in July 1563, remembering his family at the end sufficiently to leave Honychild to Elizabeth absolutely, and his lands in Chart to Roger her son; while to his step-daughter Margaret Dering he left £400.

From what may be deduced, Vaughan's character does not leave much to admire. He seems to have been ambitious and to have had a talent for organization, but he was vain and greedy, paying little attention to his wife and family, so we are left with a sense of his ingratitude to Elizabeth at the end of his career. He must have proved a source of great disappointment to her and must also have given her cause for much anxiety during the short and hectic life they led together. There could have been little happiness, nor were there any children of the marriage. We must regard this alliance as one of the least carefully undertaken actions in her life, nor is it surprising that when she resolved to marry again for the third time she made a very different choice.

In 1564 Elizabeth decided upon yet one more matrimonial venture. Her third and last husband, Sir Thomas Golding, Kt., was a worthy man and of proper dignity, for on the occasion of their marriage at Great Chart in May of that year 'he paid 45/- to the parson and clerk for their services'. He promised to be of a quieter disposition, more suitable to his wife's mature age and could offer her a safer subsistence.

According to Morant, Sir Thomas was of Belchamp St. Paul in Essex and was 'one of the Commissioners for certifying the Chantry lands in Essex, and he knew how to improve that opportunity by getting a very large share of them. He was sheriff of Essex and Herts. in 1561 and of Essex alone in 1569'.

Although there is a distinct tang of uncharitableness in the historian's sentiments regarding him, we may infer that Elizabeth, in her advancing years and experience, found a good steady man who would be likely to help her administer Roydon and her estates in comfortable security. This benefit, however, was of short duration, for he died in 1571 without any children. Elizabeth, Lady Golding, survived him many years, and we may imagine this intelligent woman in her old age devoting much time to piety and good works amongst her tenants and the poor people of Peckham.

Her son Roger, married to Ann Wyatt, daughter of the leader of the insurrection, had a large family, as will be seen at the end of this chapter. Roger had by this time taken the burdens of administration upon his shoulders and Lady Golding had leisure for interesting herself in her grandchildren and particularly in the welfare and education of young William Twysden, her eldest grandson. She was much attached to her first husband's home at Chelmington, probably owing to its nearness to her daughter Margaret Dering and her family at Pluckley. Elizabeth was a frequent visitor to London, where she was wont to stay at her house in Redcross Street in the parish of St. Giles, Cripplegate. She appears often to have transacted business there, for in 1590 her brother-in-law, Arthur Golding, of Little Birch in Essex, acknowledges a loan 'from his very good sister-in-law the Lady Golding', and in May 1591 her son Roger 'became bound to pay £60 in November of that year to Katherine Delahaye of Wateringbury, Widow (probably of his first cousin), at the house of Dame Elizabeth Golding in Redcross Street'. From the fragments of records, by her own acts and through the personalities of her three husbands, a fairly accurate picture of Elizabeth and her character may be formed. Energy, astuteness, and sound judgement, with one notable exception, can be traced in her, and, added to these, an amiability and charm of manner may perhaps fairly be claimed without over-taxing the imagination.

Elizabeth was laid to rest in Peckham Church after her death at the ripe age of 72, and in her memory a dignified monument was erected close to the chancel door, the inscription upon which reads thus:

> Here Lieth buryed Dame Elizabethe
> Goldinge one of the daughters and
> Heyres of Thomas Roydon and Marga-
> rett Wheatenhall. Wife first to
> William Twysden, after to Cuthbert
> Vaughan, Esquires, lastlie to Sr Tho-
> mas Golding Knight. Who had issue
> by William Twysden Roger and Mar-
> garett wyfe to Richard Dering of
> Pluckley. She died of the age 72
> 19 Aug. 1595.

The following letter from Mr. Anthony Wingfield to Elizabeth, Lady Golding, asking for a loan of seven pounds to enable him to proceed overseas to join Sir Philip Sidney's expedition in the Low Countries, was also among the Twysden family papers at Roydon. We reproduce the letter in full, together with the bond accompanying it, because of the quaintness and extravagance of the language which the borrower thought it necessary to use in those days when making what to us would seem a very modest request. However, the proper equipment of a young officer of Elizabeth's time would in our money have cost thirty to forty pounds and the sum asked for would probably have then approximated that amount.

Soldiering as a profession was a highly speculative

career and sometimes led to rapid and considerable wealth. Sir Philip Sidney and his friends in the Low Countries were seizing the money sent by Spain into Flanders to subsidize their allies, and rich prizes were forthcoming for all ranks taking part in a successful enterprise. Mr. Wingfield no doubt felt confident about being able to keep his part of the bargain and repay Dame Golding at the due date.

'Good Madam,

'For y^t I shoolde bee ashamed to solicitt myn own sute unto yowe, havinge never been able to deserve any favor of yowe, cawseth mee to present ye same unto yowe herby wch I knowe can not blushe. I am presently to departt to Sr Phillip Sidney, I hope to my great preferment, for y^t him self hath assured mee so mutche, but, as I have been kept from goinge with him by want, so, in my dispatchinge after him I have fownd so many impediments, as I have been forced to spend above my expectation, and am therefore constreyned to crave favor contrary to myn own desyre, where I can deserve little; yet sinc neede hath no lawe, I hope your La will both pardon my boldness, and do mee so mutch plesure as to lend mee vij^{li} till our ladye daye, wch I assure you shall bee in deed so great a pleasure, as it shall bynd me allways to bee most redy to do you any service I maye, and do herby protest before God and yowr La, y^t itt shall bee payd att y^t daye w^{t}howt all fayll, otherwyse, think mee ye most unthankfull man, and least deservinge sutch a frend, for y^t both your La kyndes shall bynd mee, and ye place wherunto I am preferred shall inable mee therunto. I beseetch your La not to deny mee herin, sinc ye great hope I have of your La hellp hathe assured mee to adventure thus farr. I mean to take by leve of you ere my departure, wch shall bee ye speedyer and better by your La, if itt will plese you to hellp mee thus farr, which I pray you immagin to bee as great a good turn as you coold do to any; for that my dispatch standeth herupon. So I humbly tak my leve, the 1 of December, 1585.

Your La most assured,
ANT. WINGFELLDE.

To ye ryght woorshipfull
   his very good lady, y^e
   Lady Golldinge.'

Enclosed is this bond:

'Bee it known unto all men by these presents, y^t I, Anthony Wingfelld, of Blankney, in ye Cownty of Lincolln, gent, do owe unto ye Lady Elysabeth Goldinge, of Royden Hall, in Pekham, in ye county of Kent, ye soom of vij^{li} of lawfull mony of Ingland, to bee payd at or before ye feast of ye anuntiation of ower Lady next cominge; for ye trew payment wherof I do, by these presents, bynd mee, myn heyrs, executors, and assingnes. In witness whereof, I have sett to my hand, the third daye of December, in ye xxviijth yere of ye reynge of our Sovereyne Lady Elysabeth, by ye grace of God, etc., a^o 1585.

By mee,

ANT. WINGFELLDE.'

Roger Twysden's epitaph is inscribed on a tablet above his tomb in East Peckham Church.

'Here lyeth buried Roger Twysden Esqr and Ann his wife D^r to Sir Th. Wyat K^t. Although they were born in the same day yet died they severally, Ann in June and was buried the sixt, An^o 1592 aged 50 current, Roger in Novr and was buried the ninth, An^o 1603 aged 61 current. . . . They had between them 12 children six died without issue and six remayned after them livinge—William, Thomas, Charles sons, Elizabeth, Margaret, Jane daughters—Charles yet unmarried the other all married have issue.'

Wm. Twysden his son erected this memorial to him in 1611.

THE WYATTS

Sir Thomas Wyatt of Allington, son of Sir Henry Wyatt, was a Privy Councillor to Henry VIII and was much favoured by him. He followed a romantic career and has been accorded by posterity the poetic laurels of his time; he travelled in Italy to study the art of poetry and letters and is thought to have made a speciality of writing in the Petrarchan form of sonnet for he wrote much in English in that measure. He was charmed with Anne Boleyn, to whom much of his poetry was dedicated, and his attachment to her became unfortunate when the King himself grew enamoured of her. Owing to this, Wyatt temporarily lost the patronage of his royal master and was confined to prison in the Tower, but was afterwards restored into the King's favour. He died in 1543/4, seized of the Mote and other property in and around Maidstone, in addition to Allington Castle.

He had only one son, Sir Thomas Wyatt, Kt., the younger, who raised the rebellion and was executed in 1553/4. In 1550 Edward VI had granted him the Manor of Maidstone, but on his attainder, the Mote and all his other properties were confiscated by the Crown (Mary R.). Allington itself was granted later to John Astley, Master of the Jewel House to Queen Elizabeth.

Extract from the Parish Records of East Peckham. 1539, Grants, 20th November:

'To Sir Thomas Wyatt, the elder; grant in tail Male to the Lordships & Manors of East Peckham and all possessions in East Peckham which came to the Crown by the gift of Thomas, late prior of Christchurch. (On account of the Dissolution of the Monasteries.) Rent £12 by way of Tenth.'

CHAPTER VI

THE TWYSDENS

WE have seen how the Twysdens, through the marriage of William Twysden of Chelmington to Elizabeth, heiress of Thomas Roydon, came to be possessed of the Manor of Roydon and its tenements. We find them at the beginning of the seventeenth century established as an old family with branches in several parts of Kent. We have already related that Elizabeth's son, Roger Twysden of Roydon, married Ann, eldest daughter of Sir Thomas Wyatt the younger, of Allington, the notorious leader of the rebellion. But in Queen Elizabeth's reign his family received back much of their lands and their prestige seems to have recovered. We have little doubt that the marriage of Roger and Ann obtained the royal assent even if it was not looked upon with favour, for it is recorded that in 1593, just after Ann's death, Roger received a grant of land from the Queen. He died in 1603, after barely eight years of succession, and his son William, the eldest survivor of twelve children, stepped into his appointments and soon occupied an even more prominent position in the county than his father had held.

William Twysden had an upbringing which qualified him to be a scholar and, in due course, a soldier and a courtier. In 1597 he took part in the Island Voyage, and in 1603 was chosen to accompany James I into London when he came from Scotland to take possession of the English Crown. He found favour at the hands of his royal master and became Gentleman Usher to the Privy Chamber, being knighted by the King at the Charter House on May 11th, 1603. In 1611 upon the creation of the Order of Baronets, Sir William was included, and in 1619 he had the honour to be one of the canopy bearers at the funeral of Queen Anne of Denmark.

Sir William had a learned education with an understanding of the classics and a knowledge of Hebrew. He founded the valuable collection of manuscripts and books at Roydon which he was 'pleased to make useful to the public'. The general subjects of this collection were a number of rare and early works on the defence of the Protestant religion and the ancient laws and Constitution of England; owing to the great scarcity of books and the comparatively few learned people of that time, Twysden's library was no doubt intended by him to be a centre of local study and research. It was to lay the foundation of the famous literary works of his son.

He married Anne, eldest daughter of Sir Moyle Finch,[1] of Eastwell in Kent, and they had four sons and three daughters, the eldest of whom, born in 1597, was named Roger after his grandfather. Sir William died in Redcross Street in 1628/9, having much improved Roydon and added to its estates.

Roger Twysden (1597–1672) was educated at St. Paul's School and Emmanuel College, Cambridge. Chalmers[2] tells us that he was a man of great accomplishments, well versed in the learned languages and exemplary in his attachment to the Church of England. He made many important additions to his father's library, which seems

[1] The Twysdens were thus connected with this important Kent family. Sir Moyle Finch of Eastwell was the eldest son of Sir Thomas and Lady Catherine Finch, and their daughter Anne married William Twysden of Roydon in 1591. The Dean of St. Paul's, Alexander Nowel, officiated at their wedding. Anne died in 1638.

Eastwell was one of the lordship manors of Romney Marsh and passed through George Finch to the Finch-Hattons, together with the titles of Viscount Maidstone and the Earl of Winchilsea and Nottingham. Hasted tells us that it came about in this way: 'Eastling in the Hundred of Faversham was granted to Sir Thomas Moyle, Kt., of Eastwell and he had an only daughter Catherine who was his heiress and married Sir Thomas Finch, Kt. (died in 1563). She married as her second husband Nicholas St. Leger, who in her right presented to the Rectory of Eastling in 1574. Her son Sir Moyle Finch, by her first husband, later succeeded to this rectory. He died in 1614, leaving his widow Elizabeth (daughter of and heir to Sir Thomas Heneage, Kt.) surviving, and she became possessed of it in 1617. She was a very distinguished lady and was created by James I, in the 21st year of his reign, Viscountess Maidstone, and later by Charles I Countess of Winchilsea in her own right; through her Eastwell descended to the Finch-Hattons, who stood possessed of it in 1769.'

[2] *General Biographical Dictionary*, by Alexander Chalmers, F.S.A.

seldom to have been neglected by his family or his descendants.

He assisted John Phillipot, Rouge Dragon, in his *Visitation of the County of Kent* taken in 1619 (*Villare Cantianum*), and that gentleman returns him acknowledgements as a person to whom 'For his learned conduct of these his imperfect labours, through the gloomy and perplexed paths of antiquity and the many difficulties that assaulted him, he was singularly obliged.'

Phillipot, mentioning the manors and demesnes within East Peckham, refers to Roger Twysden as

'The instant Lord of the Fee, a person upon whom I need drop no other character when I say that in these times, when there is such a damp and astonishment, by publick blastings and discouragements, cast upon literature, he is both a gentleman and a scholar'.

'Sir Roger Twysden obtained a Charter of "Free Warren" from the late King Charles to reduce a certain proportion of ground into a Park, which is the one the House is surrounded by at present, though the House owes much of its magnificence and splendour to the care and expense of his grandfather, Roger Twysden Esq. and his father, Sir William Twysden, Kt. and Bt.'

Roger, then aged 32, succeeded to Roydon in 1629, and occupied himself much in building and planting and otherwise improving the estate. Kemble[1] says:

'For some years after his father's death, Sir Roger Twysden lived quietly at Roydon or in London with his mother. His rent books and journals give proof that he adequately discharged the duties of landlord such as they were in far more patriarchal times than these. Not a stick of timber on the estate but Sir Roger knows its real value; not a shaw to be cut, or an oak to be felled but he is on the spot to enforce the covenants of his leases and guard the interests of his tenants, as well as his own.'

He married in 1634/5 Isabella, daughter of Sir Nicholas

---

[1] *Certaine Considerations upon the Government of England*, by Sir Roger Twysden, Kt. and Bt., edited from the unpublished manuscript with an Introduction by J. M. Kemble, M.A., Camden Society Press, 1849.

THE HALL IN ROGER TWYSDEN'S TIME
showing original door-frame and panelling in the screens (Restored)

Saunder, of Ewell in Surrey. Her family was descended from Thomas of Woodstock, and we shall give an account in her husband's own words of her great charm and ability. No man had a more loving and dutiful wife throughout circumstances of great adversity and distress.

At the beginning of the struggle between King and Parliament in 1640 we find Sir Roger Twysden living at Roydon and enjoying his estates. At a time when a great social change was taking place throughout the kingdom, profoundly affecting the country squire, the Twysdens stood for the King, the Realm, and the Church. The passing of the feudal lord of the Middle Ages had proceeded rapidly during the Elizabethan era. The progress of culture and learning, the improvement in printing,[1] the expansion of trade and colonization, the growing depth of feeling and colour in political thought, all urged upon the landed gentleman of the time a far wider responsibility than was demanded of the old lords of the manor in the circumscribed world of their day.

Sir Roger Twysden was one who was inevitably influenced by these tendencies, throwing himself wholeheartedly into the troubled questions of his day. Regular attendance at the Bench as a county magistrate, and the many influential people he met there, gave him an insight into the political situation and kept him in touch with it.

He was elected member for the county of Kent in the Short Parliament, but his tenure of the seat was of short duration, for Sir Edward Dering of Pluckley, his second cousin, was elected to the Long Parliament in his place the same year.

What would have happened if Twysden had been re-

---

[1] Hadlow, a village in the Weald only three miles west of Peckham Church, lays claim to be the birth-place of William Caxton, the great typographer of the fifteenth century. He himself recorded that he was born in the Weald of Kent, and we find in the parish of Hadlow the small Manor of Causton to have been possessed by the de Caustons in the fourteenth century. If we accept the broad pronunciation of the Weald folk in those days as a fact (viz. 'Haudloo' for Hadlow, 'Mauling' for Malling, and countless other examples), we may infer that the de Caustons were *Caxtons*, and William Caxton one of the family. (*Arch. Cant.*, vol. ii, Misc., p. 232.)

elected to the Long Parliament? Was he prepared to go to the necessary lengths? Probably he was not, and therefore, no doubt, he refrained from seeking re-election.

As a writer of outstanding ability he had more than a good claim to a profound knowledge of the affairs of Church and State and of constitutional law. He was outspoken to a degree bordering on indiscretion, and it was inevitable in the circumstances that he made enemies who later gloried in the discomfort to which he was put. Moreover, his legal knowledge was enough in itself to bring upon him a certain amount of odium and distrust as to how he might use it, and there is no doubt that the fear in which he was held by his enemies, lest their summary ordinances should suffer overthrow at law, was largely the cause of the treatment he received and the prolonged period of oppression and injustice that he was forced to endure. Although far from being what we call to-day a Socialist, he was wedded to the cause of social betterment. All his efforts were aimed at securing freedom and peace so that the best in men might be devoted to a pious and useful life. He stood for progress by development, and for building on to the existing order of things rather than tearing them down by violence and bloodshed; he believed, too, as do the best political elements of our own times, that the newly awakened desire for better conditions, both in government and in the Church, could be more successfully achieved by gradual improvement than by the forces of disruption.

Yet at this period of crisis England was being cleft into extremes. Abell[1] says:

'In reviewing the condition of England at this time, we are continually reminded that moderation of any kind was intolerable—from moderation in matters of religion to moderation in the matter of dress. There were, of course, some men of the moderate stamp of Twysden who were so far ahead of their age as to condemn the excesses of their own party as emphatically as those of the other, but the ordinary man in the street

[1] *Kent and the Great Civil War*, by H. F. Abell.

was an extremist. If he was a Puritan and the position of an altar displeased him, he wrecked the Church. . . . As in every-day life, so in his politics he was an extremist, and from the position of a sturdy, right and broadminded upholder of the common rights of free men, developed into a bigoted tyrant who denied any rights whatever to men of an opposite political or religious creed. The Cavalier was just as bad and made it a study to go to the opposite extreme of the Puritan in all things. The result was that however deep the sympathies of some of us may be with the picturesquely attired, sad-faced, gentlemanly King, we cannot be blind to the fact that the majority of his followers were as big blackguards in everything but name and birth as the men who fought in the Wars of the Roses or the Feudal Barons who preceded them.'

Twysden himself lived in surroundings of wealth and beauty, with no greater desire than to remain planted firmly in the constitutional soil of the land. Such a tradition unquestionably carried with it loyalty to the King and the Protestant Church, and it is not to be wondered at that Roger, in the prime of life, with ideals such as these, qualified by a brilliant and active intellect, was involved in the troubles of the landed gentry of his time.

Twysden's principles were in fact the very root of the issues which were to be so bitterly fought out. They were far more subtle than the mere issues as between one class and another, for indeed all classes were represented on both sides in the Civil War. The lower orders fought with the gentlemen they knew and trusted.

But the two main issues themselves—the King's Divine Right and the deep cleavage in the Church—were questions little understood except by the better educated and deeper-thinking men of the time, of whom Twysden was a good example. He saw the menace to the religion of the Protestant Church caused by the attempt to abolish the right to worship as men pleased, and by the compulsory substitution of Archbishop Laud's New Prayer Book. The people did not need logic: their feelings were intui-tive, and Twysden sensed with unerring instinct the advent of a profound upheaval that manifested itself to

G

an ever-increasing degree in those years immediately pre-
ceding the outbreak of the Civil War. Abell again says:
'So long as Parliamentary Supremacy meant a check on
Royal Tyranny, Kent was for the Parliament; but when
Parliament called into existence a power which it could
not control, and another sort of Tyranny was exercised,
Kent returned her allegiance to the King.'

The Petition of Kent in 1642, with which Twysden was
closely associated, if indeed he was not the actual author
of it, was a powerful warning, which, however, failed to
avert the Attainder of Strafford, the councillor to whom
the King was most indebted, and to prevent the deplor-
able episode of the attempt to seize the five members on
the floor of the House of Commons. Such hasty and un-
constitutional display only betrayed the more readily the
inner weakness of the monarch at a moment when his very
throne depended on the correct appraising of the temper
of his subjects and their powers of further endurance.

There was nothing treasonable in the petition itself, yet
it was seized upon and proclaimed as such by those who
were afraid of its possible influence not only in the county
of Kent but throughout the kingdom. The threats against
Twysden's person were instigated largely by the local
administration in Kent on account of its fear of his
authority through and beyond the county itself, partly also
because of the jealousy of his personal enemies. Even so,
it was some considerable time before Twysden could bring
himself to believe that his estates were really sequestered.
An expert in matters of law, he failed to see how any legal
proceedings, which made lawful an act of pure robbery,
could be carried out even if it could be justified.

Abell defines the process of sequestration as follows:

'A man's estate was seized; he would sue to find out what
crime he had committed. Parliament would equivocate and
postpone enquiry, in the meantime that their agents would
receive rents, fell timber, pass as owners of the estate until to
get off absolute ruin, the real owners would actually own
themselves offenders, and make composition for their own

estates, that is, pay a lump sum down and be freed from further annoyance and robbery. Possibly a more iniquitous and barefaced scheme for raising money was never put into practice, even by a religious power.'

Twysden was first arrested immediately after the issue of the petition, and held prisoner in London at Covent Garden pending examination. After his arrest 'it was resolved in the House that Sir Roger Twysden and Sir George Strode be put out from the Commissioners for the County of Kent, named in the Bill of Scandalous Ministers upon this question, April 7th, 1642'.

Shortly afterwards he procured bail, on his bond not to enter into the county of Kent beyond ten miles from London, but this restriction was later relaxed and he returned to Roydon on May 17th, 1642, bound only to appear if called upon.

He unwisely repaired to the next assizes at Maidstone and, again incurring the displeasure of the Committee for Kent, was arrested on August 5th, and sent to the 'Three Tobacco Pipes' in Charing Cross. After a fortnight, however, he was allowed to go to his town house in Redcross Street, where he spent the winter. It was during this winter that he gave much time to his literary works, preparing his manuscripts and writing them in his own hand.

In May 1643 he sent his young son William to France with his tutor, Mr. Hamnet Ward, making up his mind to slip away quietly afterwards and follow them. Conceiving his arrest to have been illegal and without warrant, he ignored his undertaking for the grant of bail and was discovered in disguise at Blackheath when on his way to take ship at Greenwich. He was arrested, and this time sent to the 'Counter' at Southwark, where he was kept in much stricter confinement, and it was not until the following February (1644) that his brother-in-law, Sir Christopher Yelverton,[1] was able to procure him an exchange to

---

[1] Sir Christopher Yelverton, Bt., of Easton Maudit, Northamptonshire, was son of the distinguished Sir Henry Yelverton. He married Anne, younger sister of Sir Roger Twysden. She died in 1670, aged 67.

Lambeth, where he endured more comfortable conditions. Here, during the next two years, he wrote much of the *Decem Scriptores*.[1]

He decided on total submission in 1645, and entered into a composition for his estate, released in the sum of £1,500 (instead of £3,000 originally). He finally paid about £1,300 and returned to Kent in January 1650, broken in fortune and spirits, to find his estate wasted, his woods cut down, his tenants dispossessed, and all his cherished plans of improvement and ornament rendered vain. He spent his later years in trying to repair the damage, but even during this time his house was constantly subjected to search by the army for hidden papers and documents. In 1651 they carried him and his brother-in-law, Sir Hugh Cholmley, as prisoners to Leeds Castle. He was released soon after, but Cholmley was kept there for two months.

Roger Twysden had refused to pay Ship-Money to Charles I and declined to lend money to the Long Parliament. After the Restoration he threw up the deputy-lieutenancy which had been conferred upon him, rather than burden the militia with coat money, for providing the men with uniforms as well as arms, a measure which he considered to be an unfair imposition.

Although his political record was well known, he was spared, on account of his years, any outward sign of the displeasure of the Cabal Ministry, for by this time he had retired to the seclusion of Roydon, there to spend the remainder of his life. Nevertheless, he attended the Bench regularly, and it was while riding through Malling Wood on his way to Petty Sessions on June 27th, 1672, that he fell from his horse in an apoplectic fit and died, in the seventy-fifth year of his age.

[1] Sir Roger Twysden's Works: (1) *Treatise on Usury*. (2) An Account of Queen Anne Bullen. MS. (3) *Certaine Considerations upon the Government of England*. (4) *The Commoner's Liberty or the Englishman's birthright*. (5) *Historiae Anglicanae—Decem Scriptores*. (6) *Historical vindication of the Church of England in point of Schism as it stands separated from the Roman and was reformed I Elizabeth*. (7) *Increase of the Papal Power in England. How far the Regal Power did extend itself in Matters Ecclesiastical*. (8) A Catalogue of MSS. (9) *Sir Roger Twysden's Diary*.

Thus Kemble sums up Sir Roger's attitude in the difficult circumstances of his generation:

'Loyal, yet not a thorough partisan of the King; Liberal, yet not prepared to go to all lengths with the Parliament: an earnest lover of the Church of England (as it existed under Elizabeth, not under Laud), yet anxious for a conciliation with Rome: a careful manager, yet an indulgent landlord: a somewhat stern and humorous man, yet a devoted son and husband and affectionate father—such is the picture of a man who even to this day excites in us feelings of respect and attachment.

'The history of the Civil Wars can only be thoroughly understood when we have obtained a wider insight than we yet possess into the objects and views of the country gentlemen of England at that time. These are now to be sought only in the private records of their families and I trust that by degrees they will be permitted to our study.'

In view of the data we have at our disposal, mainly from the pen of this learned gentleman himself, we propose to devote a somewhat disproportionate amount of space to a relatively short period, and to give an account in following chapters of his adventures and persecutions, to show how deeply Roydon was affected by the uncertainties of politics and the upheavals of the great Civil War.

His son William, the third Baronet (1635–97), succeeded him. He distinguished himself in the Parliament of James II, but retired early from the political arena to devote his time to Roydon. There is no doubt that it was he who carried out the considerable additions and improvements to the house and garden which we notice in a later chapter.

Sir Roger, as we have mentioned before, was the eldest son of a large family. He had several distinguished brothers, of whom Thomas achieved considerable eminence as a barrister at law and became one of the Justices of the King's Bench after the Restoration, for which he was given a baronetcy. He founded the branch of the family which settled at Bradbourne,[1] near East Malling, rebuilt

[1] p. 60.

by one of his descendants in 1714. It is one of the most beautiful of the lesser early Georgian mansions in England, and its late owner, Sir John Twisden, a direct descendant, until recently resided there.

The other member of this family, of whom some account must be included, is the second child and eldest daughter. Elizabeth Twisden[1] was born in 1600 and married Sir Hugh Cholmley, Bt., of Whitby in Yorkshire. At her death in 1655 she chose to be buried in the family vault in East Peckham Church, and there is a tablet in memory of her daughter and herself on the north wall of the Church which reads as follows:

'To the memory of Mistress Elizabeth Cholmeley, daughter of Sir Hugh Cholmeley, of Whitby in the County of Yorkshire, and Elizabeth his wife, daughter of Sir William Twysden, Kt., Bt., who according to her own desire was laid near the Remains of her Parents from whom she did not degenerate, being a very worthy Person and of a Pious and Virtuous life. She[2] dyed ye 14th of November in ye yeare of Our Lord 1699.'

The Cholmleys were a branch of the Cholmondeleys of Cheshire, and settled near Whitby Abbey in the North Riding of Yorkshire towards the end of the fifteenth century. There was a Sir Richard, famous in Yorkshire annals as the 'Black Knight', who was the great-grandsire of Sir Hugh Cholmley born in 1600.

The latter wrote his *Memoirs*, published by his descendant, Nathaniel, in 1789, and so closely does the narrative relating to the period of the Civil War resemble in style the journal of Sir Roger Twysden that the fact would be surprising had they not become near relations by marriage. But the Cholmleys also owned lands in Kent, and no doubt this was how the two families originally came into contact.

These two fellow sufferers of the Civil War evidently

---

[1] Elizabeth Twisden's, Lady Cholmley's, portrait, which is reproduced, hangs at Howsham Hall, owned by Mrs. Willoughby to whom it has descended, though several times the property has passed through the female line.
[2] The daughter.

ELIZABETH TWISDEN
afterwards Lady Cholmley

had much in common. Their circumstances were substantially the same, although considerable distance separated them. Sir Hugh inherited a much impoverished estate, and his father, when only 24, was forced to come to an arrangement with him, granting his son a lease of the property in consideration of an annuity of £400 per annum. In 1641 Hugh was created a baronet, and by the date of his father's death, through the most stringent economies, he had paid off much of his indebtedness.

At the outbreak of the Civil War Cholmley, like Twysden, was moved by a similar inspiration and torn by the same struggle between his loyalty to the King and his desire for progress in the affairs of government.

His tenets compare so closely to those of Twysden himself that we cannot help believing that they met frequently to discuss their political opinions and mutual grievances, a fact that would not seem strange owing to their close friendship.

Sir Hugh was forcibly removed from his commissions upon refusal to pay the King's levy of Ship Money, holding in contempt, like all honest squires, what he considered was a corrupt and extortionate imposition, and a dishonour to the nation. Therefore, in the first part of the Civil War he is found supporting the standard of Liberty, and after very reluctantly deciding to take up arms, he was instrumental in securing Scarborough Castle, in November 1642, for the Parliament forces. He was soon impressed, however, with the royal successes and his conscience began to disturb him. He was probably of the opinion that the King would speedily be successful and proceed at once to redress the wrongs of the people, and so in the following year (1643) when the King's star was still in the ascendant, he is discovered upholding the Royal Standard as Governor for the King in Scarborough Castle, which he most gallantly defended for over a year. Later, when the tide turned strongly in favour of the Parliament forces, further resistance became useless, and he was forced to surrender in July 1645.

He obtained his liberty to proceed to France and returned later, after agreeing to compound for his estate in Yorkshire, but did not survive to see the Restoration.

Elizabeth Cholmley was a devoted wife and remained with her husband throughout these troubled times, even enduring the hardships of the siege of Scarborough Castle. She had a very charming disposition, to which there is a tribute in Sir Hugh's own account from the *Memoirs*:

'She was of the middle stature of women, and well shaped, yet in that not so singular as in the beauty of her face, which was but of a little model, and yet proportionate to her body; her eyes black and full of loveliness and sweetness, her eyebrows small and even as if drawn with a pencil, a very little, pretty, well-shaped mouth, which sometimes (especially when in a muse or study) she would draw up into an incredible little compass; her hair a sad chestnut; her complexion brown, but clear, with a fresh colour in her cheeks, a loveliness in her looks inexpressible; and, by her whole composure, was so beautiful a sweet creature at her marriage as not many did parallel, few exceed her, in the nation.'

This vivid picture in writing of a much-beloved wife bears close resemblance to Roger Twysden's uplifting tribute of praise to the character of his own wife Isabella, in a beautiful and moving passage written after her death:

'Isabella Saunder, daughter of Sr. Nicholas Saunder, of Ewell, in Surrey, by Nonesuch, marryed to me the 27th. day of January, 1634/5, mother of six children, three male and three female . . left the miseries of this life at a little house of myne in ye Dean's Yard, in a little court in Westminster, the 11th. day of March, 1656/7, about 6 of ye clock in ye after noone, or rather not so much, but very nigh ye houre, the day on which she dyed beeing Wensday, and was brought downe and buried by my father in our little burying place, (in the Chancel) in East Peckham Church, ye Tuesday following, beeing ye 17 day of March 1656/7.

'She was a person of the most virtue and fewest vices I ever saw. She was truly religious and fearing God, serving hym allwayes in spirit and truth, after the auntient manner of the English Church, as it was reformed by Queen Eliz. and King James. This seasoned all her other actions and made them such as were acceptable in yᵉ sight of God and good men. She had a very discerning judgment, and wᵗʰ that, a temper beyond imagination, and, with it, an affectionate nature to all, especyally such as loved her or me, of whom, if that can bee a fault, she was too fond, and so of her children. With that patience she, for my sake, endured the loathsomeness of a most nasty pryson, called yᵉ Counter, in Southwark, that she might have my company onely; with what wisdom she sollicited, then and afterward, my business at Committees, and at the howse of Commons, sometymes, itself; with what magnanimyty she went through those miserable tymes, (in wᶜʰ it was enough to be undone, not to bee so foolysh as not to consent or run madly to our owne ruine, yᵗ beeing the undoubted mark of a MALIGNANT) I shall not heere write, because indeede I have not words to expresse it.

'She was not at all unwilling to dye, insomuch as when she, growing weaker, my Cosen Burraston told her she feared "she was not a woeman" she took the words out of her mouth, and added herself, "of this world;—God's will bee done; hys name be ever praysed!"

'I was, unfortunately, in yᵉ Country, when she fell sick of her last sickness. She had been ille of a Cold; but was prety well recovered agayn; but yᵉ night I went away was stricken with death; though they conceived it onely a Cold. On Tuesday yᵉ 10 March, they sent a messenger of purpos for me. I saw there was then no delaying; but went so early, as I was wᵗʰ her about 10 of yᵉ clock, found her much spent, her eyes to have lost her naturall quicknesse. Yet God gave her then a little lightning before death: Was joyd to see me, received the sacrament VIATICUM with me, wᶜʰ done, she kissed the Minister, and us about her, to take her leave of us,—told me wee should meete in heaven. I never saw any receive the Eucharist wᵗʰ more reverent devotion. Then, growing neerer her end, desired to bee layd to rest again, beeing heavy as nigher her tymes end. About 3 of the clock, she awaked agayn, knewe me. I kist her and she me; but I could not well understand her speech, but, as I since conceive it was, yᵗ she might dye quyately, wᶜʰ she did, laying her self again to sleepe; but never waked more in this world.

'When I kist her, which was yᵉ last I ever did whilst she lived, she gave me many kisses together, so as I told her, "heere is yᵉ old kisse still". She smiled, as what she knewe she used to doe.

'She was of a weak constitution, very sickly, in so much as some tymes jesting wth her, and saying in sport, not long beefore her end, "If God ryd me of this, for a second wife I would take no thought", she, as conscious of her owne weaknesse, replyed, "Mock not, it may be sooner than you think;" and so it happened.

'I may not forget, after her death, she reteyned y^{t} amyable pleasing sweetnesse of countenance, she had living. I could not absteyn from kissing her to see it,—God suffering her body carry to her coffyn the lovely aspect, to show how deere and pleasing her soule was in hys sight. Lord! make me live as she lived, and truly fear God as she did, that I may dye as she did; y^{t} I may attayn that happy crown she is now in possession of.

'I may not forget, to these many guifts of mind, she had a very weak body; often sickly, or rather, allwaies sickly; often sick very desperately, at least, since her last child, Charls, seldom well. When I lay in Lambeth, eyther from the contagion of many coming into it, after the fight at Naseby, or, seeing Sr George Bunckly, whom she saw in hys extreamyty ready to depart, or anxiety of mynd to see me wth out any hope of freedom, she fel into a sicknesse, wch ended in a double quartan ague; after which, or rather perhaps her ill childbed of my yongest boy Charls, she had lesse her health then beefore; though God lent her me about 12 years after, yet ever weak.

'Her goodnesse I can not expresse, her pyety, mildnesse, temperance, not to be styrd, not at all passionate, sweetnesse of nature, judgment, justice, fellow-compassionatenesse, patience, humility, yet well understanding herself and her dwe, they who best knewe her can onely judge. Of her humblenesse I shall onely give this one example: after some of her great journeys into Kent, wch she undertooke for my buysinesse, and so very wisely sollicited, seeing her ille and great wth child, I have sometyme sayd, "What an unfortunate man am I y^{t} have brought a gentlewoeman to such a deal of mysery for my sake!" She would take me up, as intymatyng and saying she would endure much more for my sake. When I was first sequestered, I kept a man to wayt upon her; after I could not; which she was so well contented with as nothing more.

'She was the saver of my estate. Never man had a better wife,—never children a better mother.'[1]

---

[1] *Arch. Cant.*, vol. iv, pp. 199 et seq.

CHAPTER VII

SIR ROGER TWYSDEN AND THE CIVIL WAR
PART I

THERE is no more interesting document relating to the period of the Civil War than the illuminating diary of Sir Roger Twysden. It is a very human account of persecutions suffered at the hands of Parliament between the years 1641 and 1648, and the great injustice done to this worthy gentleman by the administration at Westminster through its local committee in Kent. The manuscript, beautifully written in the author's own hand, lay hidden at Roydon for many years and was only removed from there when William Cook acquired the place in 1837. Even then it did not see the light of day, nor was it until 1858, in the first volume of the *Transactions of the Kent Archaeological Society*, that it made its début to the world in serial form in that publication, much to the delight of its readers. We owe a debt of gratitude to the Society for discovering it, thereby enriching the history of Kent and our country by such a fortunate circumstance. As the Society says, the journal is a plain statement of facts left to speak for themselves. There is no attempt at distortion or exaggeration, it is a simple journal of events as they actually occurred.

The author completed the diary and prepared it for publication. The only reason he did not publish it himself is probably that he was engaged on more important constitutional and religious writings, and left his personal diary until after these were finished. He may even have intended it to be kept back until his death and published posthumously by his family, a charge which, if this was the case, they unfortunately neglected to perform. It was not until the Rev. Lambert Larking,[1] Vicar of Ryarsh,

---

[1] Lambert Blackwell Larking was the son of John Larking of Clare House, West Malling (who was High Sheriff of Kent), by his wife Dorothy, daughter of

nr. West Malling, who became, by marriage to a Miss Twysden, entitled to have access to and publish the documents, that they became available. Mr. Larking followed up his zeal and success in editing the diary by becoming the eminent Secretary to the Kent Archaeological Society itself.

Those who have read this witty and picturesque account cannot but feel they know the intimate feelings of the author himself, nor help sympathizing with his unfortunate predicament. We have not attempted to quote the diary in full but merely endeavoured to portray the writer's experiences during this time, quoting many of the most elegant passages of the diary. In doing so we have translated the text into modern English for the convenience of the reader, while keeping as close as possible to the original phraseology. We illustrate by the courtesy of the Kent Archaeological Society the facsimile of the title-page.

'The 10th May 1641 the King gave his assent to that fatal Bill for perpetuating the Parliament, soon after which the Commons began to think of barring bishops from voting in the House of Peers.

'I remember I told Sir John Finch,[1] who spake to me of it, I did fear that was but a step to take away their function; to which his answer was an assurance that there would be no considerable part of the House for that. And to speak truth, they were generally so great advancers of prerogative, (which an English Prince may better exercise than talk about), that joining with the Privy Council at sundry times, they were thought to sway the Lords, not so much with an eye for the Country's good, as the King's interest.

'The perpetuating the House I did ever look upon as similar to the action of the Thirty Tyrants of Athens, told by Xeno-

---

Sir Charles Style, Bt. Lambert married Ffrances, daughter of Sir William Jarvis Twysden, Bt. Besides inheriting the Twysden MSS. through his wife, he was presented by Sir Edward Dering, Bt., with the Surrenden MSS. He was born on February 2nd, 1797, and died August 2nd, 1868, Vicar of Ryarsh.

He planted many curious trees in the vicarage garden at Ryarsh, and his hobby of natural history is said to have been instilled into his life by an early Malling resident, John Downman, A.R.A.

[1] Note on Finch of Fordwich at end of chapter (p. 107).

AN HISTORICALL, NAR-
RATIVE of the two

howses of Parliament and either of
them, their committees and Agents
violent proceedings against Sr Roger Twysden their imprisoning his person, sequestring
his estate, cutting down his woods, and Tymber to his allmost undoing, and forcing him
in the end to Composition for his own.

Cicero Orat. 29. Pro domo sua

§. 386, n 35. Editio. Roberti Ste-
phani. Paris. MDXXXIX.

Omnis acerbitas Syllani temporis, quid maxime sit insigne
ad memoriam crudelitatis? Opinor pænam in cives Romanos
nominatim sine judicio constitutam.

Apud Tacit. Annal. 16. Capito

ut imperium ostentant libertatem præferunt: Si perverterint ipsam aggrediuntur.

TITLE-PAGE OF SIR ROGER TWYSDEN'S JOURNAL

phon, that would never end unless forced. Men in authority do not easily quit what they have once possessed themselves of, and generally look rather at what may strengthen their power than the particular good of those trusting in them, without whom perhaps they had not ascended to that position. . . . I dare boldly say there is no example in history of any temporary Court, having perpetuity attached to it, that did ever end till it was necessitated, and I think few now doubt this late Parliament would ever have set a period to their sitting, had there been a less powerful solicitor than My Lord Protector to whom this nation is infinitely bound for seeing it concluded.'

Thus begins the diary, and, in parenthesis, Twysden describes the Long Parliament as the beginning of our troubles (*initium malorum nostrorum*). Let us see how a modern historian comments upon it.

Professor Trevelyan says:

'The Long Parliament is the true turning-point in the political history of the English-speaking races. It not only prevented the English monarchy from hardening into absolutism of the type then becoming general in Europe, but it made a great experiment in direct rule of the country and of the Empire by the House of Commons. In the course of that experiment the Long Parliament successfully organised the largest military operation ever till then conducted by Englishmen in a four years' war against the King. After the victory it failed to make a permanent settlement at home, but it made England feared and honoured abroad. After all these memorable years the House of Stuart may be restored but it would never again be possible to govern the country without the participation of the House of Commons. In all the years of the Long Parliament it was the Commons who led and the Lords who followed with ever growing reluctance.'

Why did Twysden deplore the continuing of this Parliament? Probably because he saw that the last hope of safeguarding the Sovereign power lay in the King exercising it drastically and governing without a Parliament at all. Only by so doing could Charles maintain the position to which he would admit no alternative. By prolonging the session of Parliament he would have been allowing his enemies the best weapon for bringing about the slow but certain demise of Royal Absolutism. And yet was Twysden not sufficiently a constitutionalist to welcome this change, to see its inevitability and to appreciate its possible advantages? We must remember that, deep student as he was both of the law and the Church, he was also a country squire with all the interests that pertained to such a position. In the upheaval these changes were bound to bring, he saw the likelihood of losing everything he held most dear: his position, his estates, and possibly even his life.

'Some while after hearing of the perpetuating the Parliament; of the Earl of Strafford's execution by a private law and no other declaration of his treason but Mr. Solicitors argument, I cannot deny but I began to be much troubled, and resolved to seclude myself from anything of public life so much as lay in my power, remembering a saying of my fathers, "Bene vivit qui bene latet" (Safest is he who lies well hidden). And that I might give no offence, resolved as occasion should serve to go beyond the seas, for which purpose I had provided me of a pass which I kept by me.

'What troubled me about my Lord's execution was that if penal statutes, even those which concerned treason, might be expounded, not according to the letter, but by equity, I did not see that any man could be certain of not being impeached for treason.'

We do not regard his intention to go abroad as merely an ignominious attempt to evade responsibility and to secure his own personal safety. The man's outspokenness, both in his opinions and writings, rendered him incapable of being regarded as disinterested or unbiased. Nor was it easy for him—being neither an unquestionable loyalist nor a whole-hearted reformer—to escape the suspicion of being actively hostile to both sides in the dispute. Twysden's loyalty to the King, in so far as truth and tradition went, was taken for granted, but his open criticism of Charles's conduct and the state to which the King had reduced the nation's affairs showed clearly that he foresaw trouble to come and that he deemed the proper procedure for obtaining redress to be by means of, and through the observance of, the laws and the Constitution. Thus, in the view of the King's supporters, he could not be looked upon as entirely free of sympathy with the Parliamentary party, while the latter regarded him as a source of great danger by reason of his learned qualities and considerable influence locally. Twysden soon made up his mind that to remain at Roydon without being involved in the definite support of one side or the other would be impossible. Therefore he decided to absent himself in order to avoid being impaled upon the horns of a dilemma and having to declare upon which side he was ranged, a course which in his view led to certain destruction.

Presumably he thought the King was powerful enough to quell any outbreak swiftly, and that thereafter proper redress would be made. He hoped that an act of indemnity would be passed which would suffice to restore their estates to those who had been unfortunate enough to have them confiscated. Thus he writes of the changeability in the temper of government, and the uncertainty throughout the country from day to day.

'The 1st March 1641/2, both Houses did protest that if His Majesty did not give them satisfaction the dangers and distempers of the Kingdom were such, they would be enforced to dispose of the militia after the same manner as had been propounded to His Majesty, and they resolved to do it accordingly. By which men observed how easily their minds were changed, to see those very men who, in a declaration not full three months before, did avow all they had done to have been for His Majesty's greatness, honour and support; and a little after, that they had been ever careful not to have desired anything which might weaken the Crown, either in just profit or useful power; and who the 31st December, affirmed themselves ready to spend the last drop of their blood to maintain his Crown and Royal Person in greatness and glory, now to tell him they will dispose of the strength of the kingdom with him; when certainly no more useful power could appertain to Majesty than not to allow people to be punished by a law to which he does not assent, nor anything more against the honour and greatness of a monarch than to deprive him thus of the protection he owes his subjects. On these considerations, I know, many held it a thing of dangerous consequence to have men punished by order of the Houses interpreted by themselves, which I myself afterwards had sufficient experience of.'

Indeed, this is a marvellously scathing indictment of the vacillating opinions and actions of the members of both Houses of Parliament and a covert accusation against them for their disloyalty to and distrust of their monarch.

'And from hence the Royalists will have the rise of our miseries to have sprung. As, not deeming that Prince to begin the war, who first arms himself, but he that doth (and persists in doing) the first so apparent injury, that the other can have no possible way of redressing it but by force, nor any means to maintain himself and his (own) but (by) war.'

We may not only appraise this as being a concise summing up of the distempers that gave rise to the inception of the Civil War; we may also commend it to ourselves in this year of grace and to statesmen in their difficulties with foreign neighbours. There could be no more interesting commentary on the dangers of compulsory one-sided disarmament being the soil in which the germination of war may be said to thrive. Charged with the first responsibility of government, which is to govern and keep order within, Charles was threatened with an attempt by his enemies to disband the most trusted weapon for that purpose at his disposal, namely, the militia. The Parliament, on the other hand, fearing what the King might do with the power of a loyal army behind him, attempted to render him harmless first so that, in Twysden's words, nothing was left to him but to employ force as the only means to maintain himself and carry out his trust. Kemble says:

'The ordnance by which the Parliament took the command of the militia out of the King's hands completed Sir Roger's detestation of their proceedings and probably from that time caused him to express himself more openly and to concert with his friends upon means of making public protest' . . .

'But with these particulars I have not here taken upon me to meddle, further than to show in what a conjuncture of time I went to the Assizes at Maidstone, whither I came on Tuesday, the 21st March 1642, the Assize beginning the next day.'

Twysden is at great pains to describe the exact events and circumstances leading up to the meeting with his colleagues immediately before the assize. It appears that the judge on circuit was Sir Thomas Mallet. Twysden met several distinguished friends and fellow Justices of the Peace, amongst whom were Sir George Strode of Squerries (Westerham) and Sir John Sedley of St. Clere (Ightham). On the night before the session the three of them together joined at supper other friends, whom they discovered listening to a discourse by Sir Michael Livesey of Eastchurch, Sheppey. Some seemed to be taking objection to it as expressing opinions 'not in accord with the sense of the County'. The party, reinforced by Twysden, set to work to frame a petition to the Parliament and to agree there and then upon an address. It was calculated by the Parliamentary supporters to intimidate the King, who was at that time in the north, and by the royal supporters to goad the King into fresh efforts to get matters under control.

As to the question of authorship Twysden says:

'Amongst us the question grew who should draw this Petition. It was concluded (truly upon my motion) the Grand Jury should nominate some of the Bench and they some of the Grand Jury, to consider and do it. Whereupon such as were chosen from either side went together to a private lodging, I myself being of the number, where were presented to us several headings, some being approved, some corrected and others expunged. . . . Certain gentlemen were nominated to meet after supper, it being now evening, to draw them up into the form of a Petition. I was one of these but could not attend the service, being myself that night taken very ill. Going to my lodging through the *Star*[1] I met Mr. Blount of Blackheath,

[1] In the High Street of Maidstone.

H

whom I perceived not to be satisfied with our intentions, in
fact he was the only person I have seen so. That night the
Petition was drawn, but by whom I cannot for certain affirm.
The next day hearing that it was concluded I went with Mr.
Spencer[1] to the Grand Jury, desiring that such as had it with
them would show it to us, so that we might agree upon the
expressions as well as upon the headings, whereupon all to
whom the drawing of it was committed met at a private house
in the town where it was further considered and passed, not
without some alterations.'

The Petition of Kent is too well known to require more
than a fleeting reference to its contents. It consisted of
seventeen articles in which the signatories prayed King
Charles I to preserve and defend the rights of the Protestant religion and to allow the people to enjoy the sacred
liberties of the Church and the privileges of the State undisturbed, according to the law of the land and Magna
Carta. It further required that no summary ordinance be
enforced until the law implementing it should have been
enacted by Parliament. It concluded with this dignified
sentence:

'Our hopes are yet above our fears; secure them wee beseech
you. God direct and blesse your consultations for ye remoeving of all distrusts and jealousies, and for renewing that tye of
confidence and trust wch is the highest happinesse beetween a
most gratious Prince, and us his loving people.

'And you shall have the dayly prayers of your humble
Orators, ye Commons of Kent.'

Referring to the authorship of the petition, Kemble
says:

'I am greatly mistaken, nevertheless, if he was not—I will
not say, only of counsel with those that drew it—but if the
greater part of it was not actually from his own hand. The
recurrence of favourite phrases of his own is unmistakable:
and the spirit and tendency and courage of it are his beyond
question.'

---

[1] Mr. Richard Spencer of Orpington. For a list of Kentish squires see note
at end of chapter (p. 109).

It was agreed that all the gentlemen of Kent should meet at Blackheath on Friday morning at nine o'clock on the 29th April, 1642, to accompany this petition to the House and there to present it.

'This is all that passed at Maidstone, which I set down with every particular, that after times (if at least this should outlive the present age) may judge whether the offence was of that transcendency, it were fit to cause any man, not otherwise culpable, to be in sequestration (worse than a Premunire) to lie under a tedious and chargeable imprisonment. For my part I will not here call heaven nor earth to witness—for they that will not credit me otherwise, will not do it on these protestations—I saw nothing of ill in this Petition. Neither had I in assenting to it any other intention than that there might be a clear understanding between the King and the two Houses, by their complying with His Majesty, *without ever trying who was strongest*,[1] and the subject governed by laws and not by arbitrary and revocable Votes, Orders or Ordinances, which I did apprehend as a thing of great concernment. Yet what I feared, if the difference continued, might be forced upon us, and saw no possible way of preventing but by letting them understand a considerable part of the Kingdom did not like to be so ruled. . . . Yet I did not think this a petition which no man would bear exception to. There are several men, and they will have several minds whilst we are on earth, and the desires and reasons of all are to be weighed by those to whom it properly belongs to give remedy, else I know not how to give the name of a Court of Justice to a House of Commons, if it admit the desires and reasons of such only as go with their sense to be heard; but of this hereafter.'

The next day Twysden, carrying several copies of the petition for circulation amongst his friends, rode over to dine with his cousin Sir Henry Vane (the elder) of Hadlow, one of his nearest neighbours, to discuss the matter with him, afterwards going on to proffer a copy to Mr. James of Court Lodge, Ightham. The latter refused to be associated with it on the grounds that it failed to make any expressions of gratitude to the House for what they had done, 'but rather gave the gratitude to the King for

[1] Author's italics.

the laws that had been passed'. Although his objection does not seem to have carried much weight, it shows that the petition had by no means unanimous support among the local squires in Kent.

Three days after this Sir Roger Twysden was summarily arrested at Roydon by order of the House of Commons, together with some others of his friends.

'Upon the 29th March being at my house in Kent, neither expecting any such thing, I was arrested by the order of the House of Commons bearing the date of the day before, directed thus:

'To John Hunt Esq. Sergeant at Arms, attending on the said house, or his deputy,—

'By virtue of an order this day made by the House of Commons, these are to will and require you, or your deputy, forthwith to make repair to the several abodes of Sir Edward Dering, Kt. Bt., Sir George Strood, Kt., Richard Spencer, Esq., and Sir Roger Twysden, and them there and elsewhere to apprehend, and bring before the said House, as delinquents, to answer such matters as shall be objected against them, and everyone of them. And for your so doing, this shall be your sufficient warrant. Given under my hand, the 28th day of March 1642, etc.'   'WILLIAM LENTALL.'

Two days later Twysden and Sir Edward Dering were examined in front of the House and were afterwards committed to the Sergeant of the Mace and sent as prisoners to a house in Covent Garden, to be further interrogated later.

'Some may perhaps wonder why the two Houses were so transcendently incensed at this Petition? Why they laboured so earnestly finding out a plot which was never imagined? Why they took so unheard of ways in their proceedings, for whenever did the House of Commons appoint their members to join with the Lords in examining Commoners upon oath, much less such as were joining in crime against each other? Why they showed so strange partiality as to encourage petitioning in some, yet making this one a crime so heinous that a certain lawyer of the House went so far as to say there were in it things not far from treason; and another gentleman, of I dare say sincere and pious intentions, told me I did not understand the aim of the Petition, to whom I could only reply I wished the event might prove me the fool.'

On April 9th, 1642, Sir Roger procured a petition to the House of Commons for bail to appear at their request upon condition 'not to go at all into Kent, nor more than 10 miles out of London'. This was granted in the formidable sum of £20,000.

'Truly the sum was so immense I first resolved to lie by it, for who could I procure to enter into so vast an obligation?'

He obtained the sureties of Sir Robert Filmer of East Sutton and his uncle, Francis Finch, in the sum of £5,000 each, and £10,000 upon his own bond, which sureties were accepted. Although he remained under the restriction 'not to take a steppe into Kent', he nevertheless obtained his liberty to go home on May 17th.

'And returned to house, there resolving to live quietly and meddle as little as possible with any business whatsoever. Yet being a Justice of Peace and having a trial, I went to the Assizes then next following in July 1642 of which, being the last public meeting I was ever an actor in, it will be necessary to make particular mention.'

This, indeed, he does in a lengthy tract commenting upon a number of Orders in Council by the Committee of Parliament, which enjoined many celebrated and influential gentlemen, Justices of Peace for Kent, 'to use all diligence to ensure peace in the County' and suppress, by any means they thought fit to take, any actions to the prejudice of the Parliamentary authority and to deal summarily with any one suspected of designs against the influence of the Parliament. They were designated the 'Local Committee at Maidstone'.

'On Monday the 25th. July (1642) Sir Edward Hales and some others made a show of coming to the Bench; but the Court being just risen they applied themselves to the Judge, who wished what they would impart to him might be public before all the Justices of the Peace, and to that end sent to them to meet him at his lodgings after dinner. Thither the Committee soon afterwards went, Sir Henry Vane Junr.[1] being their mouthpiece, who said he had something to impart to him from the House of Commons. To which the Judge answered that he came there to administer Justice agreeable to the law; that anything concurring with that, and coming from that body, he would willingly embrace, and desired to know whether what they had to say to him might not be made public. It was replied that it should be afterwards, but they first thought fit to acquaint himself with it. Whereupon he asked "Whether it did not concern the King?" The answer was "Not more than all things pertaining to the government of the Kingdom".'

Mr. Justice Mallet and Sir Henry Vane thereupon went into private conference, as a result of which the Parliament orders relating to the appointment of the Committee of Kent were made known to the Justices of Peace,

'who the same afternoon fell into sad and serious consideration what answer was fit for them to return. One was drawn, but as that which issues from heads of differing tempers doth not ever please all. . . . I took it up, thinking only to abbreviate it for my own satisfaction, as indeed I deemed it somewhat too long. When I had done, I read it to them and I know not by what fate, it was generally so liked as, with very few words altered, it was delivered to the Committee.'

While these deliberations had been going on between the Judge and Sir Henry Vane,

'who, as Chairman of the Committee, managed the conference and spake excellently well, temperately and soberly,

---

[1] Sir Henry Vane (the younger), 1589–1654, of Fairlawne, near Hadlow, is referred to in a sonnet by Thomas Milton: 'Vane, young in years, but in sage counsel, old . . .', and by Oliver Cromwell, 'Sir Henry Vane, Sir Henry Vane; the Lord deliver me from Sir Henry Vane'. Vane, it may be remembered, was noted for his strong views and his enthusiasm for employing extreme measures on behalf of the Commonwealth. He is described as an ardent republican and an incorruptible leader of the Parliament. He suffered for it at the Restoration, when he was one of the few to be excluded from the Act of Indemnity. Bearing himself bravely (as testified by Samuel Pepys), he was executed on Tower Hill in 1660. He was buried at Shipbourne, where there is a fine memorial to him.

It was the elder Vane, father to the above, who married Margaret, sister to William Twysden the 1st baronet. She was aunt to Sir Roger Twysden, and Vane the younger was therefore his first cousin (p. 99).

there was much agitation without, and such loud acclamations were heard and such fears of stirs began to be apprehended, that the Judge told him if it went on he would be forced to adjourn the Court. And a while after, Sir Henry Vane, by command of the Committee, retired himself, and that night went home to Fairlawne. At their going, some few followed them crying "For the Parliament", but being persons neither in number or quality greatly considerable, were not, as it seemed to me, greatly regarded.'

Thus, in spite of his intention to keep out of politics, Twysden was unable to restrain himself from becoming involved. He and his two friends Strode and Spencer were required to surrender to their bail at the House of Commons on August 2nd, 1642. Twysden was sent as a prisoner to the 'Three Tobacco Pipes' in Charing Cross, where he remained a fortnight without any charge being preferred against him.

'When I came and had rendered myself to the Parliament the 5th. of August, without ever any examination I was committed to the Sergeant, who sent me to the "Three Tobacco Pipes" nigh Charing Cross, as a prisoner; where having remained about 15 days, never sent unto, charged, nor questioned in the least measure whatsoever, they finding nothing that could possibly be objected against me, one came and told me the House was willing I should go to my Brother Cholmley's[1] at Isleworth, which I absolutely refused, seeing that there would only be the need to make another request to be released from there. Only I desired I might be charged with the breach of any law, to which the answer was "In these times the House could not look at the nice observance of Law".

'Whilst I continued there I grew acquainted with two noble gentlemen, Sir Basil Brook and Sir Kenelme Digby,[2] persons of great worth and honour, who, whilst they remained with me, made the prison a place of delight, such was their conversation and so great their knowledge.

'During this my restraint, a horrid outrage was committed

---

[1] Sir Hugh Cholmley, Twysden's brother-in-law (p. 86). This was probably his house near London.

[2] Sir Kenelm Digby, 1603–65. Van Dyck painted his portrait, wearing a scarlet cloak. It hung for many years at Knole.

by Colonel Edwin Sandys,[1] and others, sent by the Close Committee, at the House of Sir William Boteler (Butler) in Teston; his servant tortured by fire, himself, then at the Wells nigh Tunbridge, on the news, flying to the King.

'This being divulged the next day, dispersed all my family in Kent; it being believed and given out that they intended to be at my house the following night. My poor wife, never strong but then exceeding weak, not yet recovered of her lying in, having placed her children with my sister Twisden,[2] full of fright and fear came up to London on horseback. The rest shifted to one place or another where they might shroud themselves; only a few servants were left to prove the extremity, who, under God's protection staying in the House, were safe.'

Again he petitioned the House, and on September 12th was allowed out once more on bail, but advised not to go into Kent, which on this occasion he wisely refrained from doing and went instead to his house in Redcross Street, intending to depart quietly to France and remain there until the trouble was over.

'During this winter that I abode in Redcross Street I had often recourse to the Tower and had the sight of sundry ancient records of Parliament there reserved, some of which I procured to be transcribed.'

There is no doubt that Twysden made valuable use of the time in studying these records, and it is perhaps fortunate for us that this coincidence gave us what might not otherwise have been available, had not Twysden been forcibly confined for a lengthy period in London.

[1] Colonel Sandys of the Parliament forces was noted for his cruelty and plundering while leading his contingent through Kent, largely to suppress the county by fear. He was a son of Sir Edwin Sandys, described as an excellent patriot 'without any falseness to his Prince', and grandson of Archbishop Sandys of York. The Colonel died at his seat, Northborne, near Deal, from a wound received at the Battle of Worcester in 1642.

[2] Wife of his brother Thomas, afterwards Sir Thomas Twisden of Bradbourne (pp. 85–6). She was a sister of Matthew Tomlinson, who commanded the guard that escorted King Charles from St. James's Palace to Whitehall. On the scaffold, Charles gave him his gold tooth-pick in remembrance of his kind demeanour towards him, which together with the Garter Ribbon, worn by the King at his execution and handed in to Tomlinson's charge, we have often seen at Bradbourne. (*Arch. Cant.* ed.)

Twysden, following the fortunes of both sides with considerable anxiety, describes the means resorted to by the parties in order to obtain money for carrying on the war and raising their respective armies.

'Thus under pretence of maintaining the religion of the Church of England, they defaced, as being superstitious or superfluous, all the antique monuments of piety and devotion; ruined the cathedrals; found means on easy terms to divide amongst themselves those lands that the Church had been so many years possessed of; denied all former rights of monarchy, yet with a protestation of defending his royal person, honour and estate; seated in themselves an absolute power of taking from the subject all he could call his own, yet professing to uphold them in their lawful rights, propriety of their goods, and liberties. With the first and second of these, as proper for the general history of the times, I will not take upon me here to meddle. Of the third, I shall remember that having got an army and finding committees ready to forward their commands in all parts, they did little by little force from the subject the greatest mass of treasure so short a time had ever expended, yet first trying how it would relish; On the 29th November 1642 they made an order for assessing such as had not contributed at all, or not proportionately to their estate, at the 20th part, although in their declaration of the previous June, they did express that no man's affection was to be measured by the proportion of the offer, thereby expressing his goodwill to the service in any proportion he chose, yet now that expression must not be less than a 20th part of his estate.'

Bitterly resenting the *ultra vires* resorted to by the local authorities for extorting moneys in every shape and form, Twysden shows how landed proprietors were put to the utmost difficulty to comply with the numerous orders and counter-orders and therefore to avoid the sequestration of their estates, without any recourse to law or appeal for proper compensation. One of the commonest impositions levied was the commandeering of timber, especially from those estates within easy reach of London, for fuelling the ever-growing armies. In the case of Roydon, this was the most injurious penalty inflicted, as we shall see later.

Twysden proceeds to lament over a new imposition to which in our own times we are now accustomed.

'They first brought in that monster "Excise", unknown to our ancestors, with so great exclamations detested in former parliaments; erected an office for regulating it, and declared on the 22nd July 1643 what should be paid for tobacco, wine, beer, strong and small, cider, perry, grocery, imported silks, furs, linens, thread and imported wire.'

This innovation had by no means an easy passage to start with, and the list of dutiable articles had to be re-vised more than once, until, with the inclusion of meat, the tax upon which began to be gravely felt by the poor people, there was a serious insurrection of the butchers of London in February 1647. This drew from the House of Commons the affirmation that nothing short of the pre-servation of the kingdom, religion, laws, and liberty of the people, would have forced the government to main-tain such a measure, nor could they find other means to draw in malignants and neutrals, 'who had endeavoured all cunning ways to evade what ye well affected had so willingly bore'.

Charles retaliated by imposing the subsidy of *Tunnage and Poundage*.[1] Twysden sums up the whole arbitrary business as follows:

'By all of which it is more than manifest, the paying an army could not take from the subject so great a mass of treasure as they forced from them; and who can doubt it, when the event proves what all good men feared, their chiefest end of raising

---

[1] 'The King, in return for the concessions he made, obtained from the Barons and Knights an unusual grant, for two years, of the ninth sheaf, lamb, and fleece on their estates; and from the burgesses a ninth of their movables at their true value. The whole Parliament, also, granted a duty of 40s. on each sack of wool exported, on each 300 wood fells, and on each last of leather, for the same term of years. But, dreading the arbitrary spirit of the Crown, they expressly declared that this grant was to continue no longer, and was not to be drawn into prece-dent. Being soon after sensible that this supply, though considerable and very unusual in that age, would come in slowly, or would not answer the King's urgent necessities, both from his past debts and his preparations for war, they agreed that 20,000 sacks of wool should be immediately granted him, and their value be deducted from the ninths which were afterwards to be levied.'—HUME (*Arch. Cant.* ed.).

one was no other but to gain a power by which they might become masters of the wealth, and appropriate to themselves the government of the Kingdom, wresting it out of those hands in which it was legally seated, and everting all laws in opposition.'

Here then is the very element of the matter, that in the exigencies of the times lay opportunities for the ruling authority to indulge in abuses hitherto undreamed of; making a bid which, if it failed, could scarcely cause more chaos than already existed, and if it succeeded, would set no limit upon the powers with which a Parliament might invest itself in times of national emergency, when the first need of the people was order, and the first need of the government was money with which to enforce it.

Thenceforward the whole face of the Constitution was to be changed.

FINCH OF FORDWICH

Lady Finch and Lady Anne Twysden (Sir Roger Twysden's mother) were first cousins. The former before her marriage was Mabella Fotherby and was mentioned in Twysden's journal as having circumvented the dire results of sequestration by hiring her husband's estates through the influence of friends in Parliament. Her husband was Sir John Finch[1] of the Mote, near Canterbury, who was selected for great honour and promotion by Charles I. Clarendon and other contemporary chroniclers have little, if anything, good to say of him, yet he succeeded for a long time in holding distinguished offices in spite of almost universal unpopularity. In March 1628/9, while Speaker to the House of Commons, he refused to put a vote of remonstrance drawn up by a number of members, and endeavoured to avoid doing so by leaving the Speaker's Chair. He was, however, forcibly held down by two members, Valentine and Hollis, being called by one of his fellow squires on this occasion, amid the tumult of the House, 'A blot upon a noble family and unworthy to be a Kentish man.' Finch became Chief Justice in 1634, and from this point of vantage vigorously supported and followed up Noy's unpopular

---

[1] Nephew of Sir Moyle Finch, note p. 77.

measure of 'Ship Money'. 'A man', according to Clarendon, 'exceedingly obnoxious to the people upon the business of Ship Money, and not of reputation and authority enough to countenance and advance the King's Service.' Finch, however, flourished in the service of the King. During the eleven years that Charles ruled without a Parliament he was created Lord Keeper (in 1639) and Baron Finch of Fordwich (in 1640), and it was not until the Short Parliament of April 1640 that his troubles came to a head, together with those of his royal master. To this Parliament Roger Twysden was returned as one of the members for Kent. As he was well known to hold strong views against the imposition of Ship Money and the extension of the assessment for this levy to the inland towns (Maidstone itself was rated at £160 per annum), it is more than probable he was chosen to represent the county in the hope that he might be able to exercise some restraining influence over his relative. This proved to be unnecessary, however, for Finch's star had already passed the zenith, and upon the assembly of the Long Parliament he was immediately impeached: (1) for forcibly influencing the judges to give their opinion in favour of Ship Money; (2) for his behaviour with regard to the Remonstrance of 1621; (3) for attempting to carry out the iniquitous Forest Laws by the enlargement of the bounds of Strafford Langton Forest in Essex; (4) for prejudicing the King against Parliament; (5) for influencing the King to dissolve his third Parliament.

He was declared a traitor, December 21st, 1640; escaped to Holland, returned at the Restoration, and died at the Mote, near Canterbury, 1660.

He lies buried under a stately monument in St. Martin's, Canterbury, on which we read: 'Here is committed to the earth, that it may return to earth, whatever was mortal of John Finch, Baron of Fordwich, of the ancient and noble family of Eastwell, whom it pleased in preference to any epitaph to have this inscribed on his sepulchral stone: "Here lies the humble servant of the best of Kings".'[1]

[1] Abell, *Kent and the Great Civil War.*

THE KENTISH SQUIRES

The following are some of the Kentish squires intimately connected with the part taken by Kent in the struggle between the King and the Parliament:

Name	Seat	Town or village	Note
Sir George Stroode	Squerryes	Westerham	
Col. Richard Spencer		Orpington	
Sir Richard Lovelace		Bethersden	
Sir Edward Hales	Hales Place	Tenterden	M.P. Queenborough.
Sir Thomas Walsingham	Scadbury	Chislehurst	M.P. Rochester.
Sir Henry Vane (Senr.)		Hadlow	M.P. Milton.
Sir Henry Vane (Junr.)	Fairlawne	Shipbourne	M.P. Hull.
Sir Francis Barnham		Boughton Monchelsea	M.P. Maidstone.
Sir Peter Wroth	Blendon Hall	Bexley	M.P. Bridgewater.
Sir Norton Knatchbull		New Romney	M.P. New Romney.
Sir Humphrey Tufton	The Mote	Maidstone	M.P. Maidstone.
Sir Edward Boyes	Bonnington	Dover	M.P. Dover.
Mr. Brown		Great Chart	M.P. New Romney
Mr. Augustine Skinner	Totteshall	West Farleigh	M.P. Kent Cty.
Sir Edward Masters		Canterbury	M.P. Cant.
Mr. John Nutt		Canterbury	M.P. Cant.
Sir John Manning (Manny)	Linton Place	Maidstone	
Sir Edward Filmer	East Sutton	Maidstone	
Sir Antony St. Leger	Ulcombe		
Mr. William Clark[1]	Ford	Wrotham	
Sir Roger Twysden	Roydon	East Peckham	M.P. Kent.
Sir Percival Ricault	The Friars	Aylesford	
Sir Thomas Wyatt	Allington	Maidstone	
Sir Edward Dering	Surrenden	Pluckley	M.P. Kent.
Sir William Clark		Hollingbourne	
Sir John Colepepper			
Sir Michael Livesey			
Sir William Compton		Erith	
Sir William Boteler (Butler)		Teston	
Sir Robert Darell	Calehill	Canterbury	
Sir John Sackville	Knole	Sevenoaks	
Mr. Blount	Barham Place	Teston	
Sir John Sedley	St. Cleere	Ightham	
Sir Jacob Astley	Baron Astley of Reading	(Inherited Allington Castle)	
Sir Anthony Weldon		Swanscombe	
Sir Richard Boys			
Sir James Oxenden			
Sir Richard Hardress			
Lord Cobham	Cobham Hall	Rochester	
Sir Thomas Colepeper		Hollingbourne	
Lord Finch of Fordwich	Fordwich	Ulcombe	
Mr. William Colepeper	Bedgebury	Hawkhurst	
Sir George Sondes	Lees Court	Faversham	
Sir Edward Monyngs		Waldershare	

[1] Clark raised a regiment at his own expense, at the head of which he was killed at Cropredy Bridge, fighting for the King, at the age of 36.

CHAPTER VIII

SIR ROGER TWYSDEN AND THE CIVIL WAR
PART II

'HAVING the Council's pass, I thought to steal over to
France without other idea than of living quietly there.
I did assure myself, and of the same opinion were as
good judgments as I could then meet with, I was within no
words of the Order of Sequestration, and hoped I might be freer
from giving offence out of the Kingdom, than in it. So, finding
a quantity of French and Portugals ready for the design, I embarked myself amongst them, desirous not to be known, if I
could avoid it, having no servant; but with men I never saw,
all strangers to me, except one only Frenchman; and beside,
I knew myself nothing favoured by some potent men then in
Kent; so was desirous to pass through that Shire as a traveller.
Thus appointed, I went from London, in the afternoon of the
9th June 1643, and came to Bromley, where the Committee
for Kent then sat. There was Sir John Sedley, Sir Anthony
Weldon, with whom our family had heretofore some disputes
(and others). I was desirous to have passed away as one of the
crowd, which I was in hope I might have done, having then,
upon some weakness in my head, wore a cap of hair, which
they had never seen me in, which having used for some time,
I left off for the troublesomeness of it, and not finding the good
I expected.

'Falling thus into their hands, I would not (I confess) tell
them at first who I was: as what then was there to compel me
to acknowledge myself to them? And what law was there then
to bar me of passing the seas, the Statute of Richard II being
repealed, and I having the Council's pass? But this was so
great an affront offered the Parliament, that Sir Anthony
Weldon said, "If I were not Sir Roger Twysden I was a rogue
and ought to be whipped".

'At Bromley, "They searched all I had in my pocket, took
away my sword, and watch, (which Capt. Skinner told me
afterwards the Council gave him and he sold into France),
some £15 in gold I had given the Frenchman to secure, think-

ing they would never take from an alien so small a sum: but seeing it lost otherwise, I acknowledged it for mine and desired to have it; but it could not be, and under that pretence, laid hold on rings of another body's; (which whether they ever restored God knows; I am sure long afterwards they were not) and sent me up a prisoner to the House of Commons with a Letter accusatory. When I came before the Committee, I complained of my usage; they on the other side demanded of me what I had given on the propositions; I told them

"Nothing: I had lost enough by the Parliament, had lain long in prison, yet was never charged with any crime."

They bade me to retire and instead of fixing ought upon me, sent me this warrant:

10. Junii 1643.

"At the Committee of Ye House of Commons for examinations 'Whereas ye House of Commons have ordered that Sr. Roger Twysden shall bee committed to prison, and have referred it to this Committee to consider to what prison he shall bee committed; It is this day ordered; that, upon sight hereof, you receive into your custody the body of ye sayd Sr. Roger Twysden, and hym safely to keepe in the Prison of the Counter in Southwarke, and not permit hym to goe out of ye same, wth out speciall order of this Committee, or Ye House of Commons'."

"John Lisle."

"To Mr. Samuell Warecoppe.
   Keeper of Ye Counter Prison
      in Southwarke".'

In these words Twysden gives an account of his comic attempt to escape and describes it too well for us to deviate from the text. The naïve excuse for being disguised in a wig is too flimsy to cover his fury and indignation at being caught red-handed with a number of inferior emigrants while trying to escape from the wrath to come. But his sense of fairness compels him to relate the unconcealed triumph of his two most hated persecutors, Sir John Sedley and Sir Anthony Weldon, to whom the situation must obviously have been one of sheer delight. Years afterwards, while realizing that his part in the adventure had been hardly a dignified one, he saw the humour of his own humiliating position. The account is scarcely as lucid as his usual style would lead us to expect, probably owing to the fact that he was too angry at the time to remember exactly what happened. It ought to have been obvious to him that with the close scrutiny that the Parliament were exercising over all parties proceeding overseas, for the very purpose of catching delinquents, that a pass, however valid it once might have been, would not long be likely to remain so, and that in any case the holder would not escape minute examination. Why was he not sufficiently well informed to know that the Committee of Kent, to each member of whom he was intimately known, were personally examining each emigrant and that there would be a poor chance of his not being recognized? To have been successful the venture would have required far more careful planning.

And so our friend was sent to prison a second time to ponder his injustices, while the Parliament party no doubt congratulated themselves on having roundly apprehended him upon such a very good pretext.

'Placed now in Southwark I began to understand my estate was sequestered. There had been some talk of it before, but my case being, as I thought, clearly outside the words of the Ordinance and so absolutely contrary to Chapter 29 of Magna Carta, I had not been much afraid; till Sir Ed. Monins, my near kinsman and good friend, came to me in prison and not only assured me I had been sequestered ever since May but besides this the Committee were complaining they could get nothing of this half year's rent, my tenants having protested they had already paid it to me.'

Again Twysden was unlucky that in the course of his recent researches among state documents and official records for the purposes of his learned writings, he was constantly incurring the suspicions of the authorities that he was a spy in the royal cause.

While at Southwark he was allowed to receive letters, but he found that correspondence with friends in France and Italy upon a wide range of subjects, mainly to do with manuscripts, was being intercepted in the belief that he was treating with foreigners to secure political or monetary aid for the Royalists.

'Being thus committed, the Diurnall (or daily Prison Log) soon after took notice of it that I carried intelligence of great consequence with me, subtly conveyed in Nut-shells. The thing I conceive arose like this: A learned physician had given me a little round ball to be worn as an antidote against infection. This I had, and as it would seem, being searched, the supposed preservative (for I never took it otherwise) was found to have lain in a Nut-shell, which for my part, as I did not know, so to this hour cannot say what ingredients it contained.'

This is an amusing sidelight upon the thoroughness which the Parliament were now beginning to apply, not only to their military organization but also to their intelligence service. Macaulay points out how lax and feeble had been the conduct of the war on the Parliament side up to this time. He says:

'The Parliamentary leaders of what may be called the first generation were inclined to half measures. They dreaded a decisive victory almost as much as a decisive overthrow. They wished to bring the King into a situation which might render it necessary for him to grant their just and wise demands, but not to subvert the constitution or to change the dynasty. . . . The war was therefore conducted in a languid and inefficient manner.'

After the first phase, when the King's successes were everywhere apparent, the leisurely Essex was superseded by Fairfax and the Parliament forces almost at once began to be handled very differently. Thus Twysden, in the unwholesome environment of the 'Counter' at Southwark, carefully weighed the relative positions and considered the probable effect upon his own affairs. He did not remain there long, for the King's successes overawed the Parliament Committee and they considered that some important personages, already under strict supervision, should be apprehended, and that others in actual confinement should be removed from the city and segregated in a mobile prison as valuable hostages and pawns in the game. Twysden, together with others, was therefore removed 'to the Shipps', and his own comment upon this action no doubt reflects the true reason for it.

'His Majesty's forces having slain Mr. Hampden, a person very considerable in the Parliament Army, on the 18th June 1643—the Yorkshire men under Lord Fairfax, defeated by the Earl of Newcastle on the 30th June—on the 13th July Sir William Waller's army worsted by my Lord Wilmot—on the 27th July, Bristol with the arms and ammunition in it yielded up to His Majesty—and no considerable body of the Parliament then in arms except those with my Lord of Essex—it was the general opinion that the King would draw towards London on the one hand and Newcastle on the other; which, had it been followed, there is no peradventure but our miseries had ended.'

Twysden is of the opinion that the possibilities of a victorious army rapidly approaching London and the probability that certain elements of disturbance in the city were ripe for giving it aid within, there was little doubt that the King, had he been guided by a wise moderation, could have made an opportunity of negotiating an honourable peace.

'I have been told by word of mouth, from one then in great authority, it was resolved in the close Committee, (for the House did nothing that was not first projected by them) that, in the event of the King marching upon London, such conditions privately determined upon should be proffered as would have been accepted.'

But to the chagrin of his supporters the King employed quite other strategy and proceeded to lay his forces around Gloucester and besiege it. This was the worst possible meat for a hungry army with a hitherto brilliant record of success. Charles made a grave error of judgement in not keeping his men stimulated and moving on towards the final objective which would decide the issue.

In front of Gloucester his army grew apprehensive and meditated upon their arrears of pay and the length of time they had been away from their homes. Dissatisfaction and impatience began to grow with increasing effect, and by the time the King had realized his mistake and abandoned the siege it was already too late. He had given the Parliament the priceless breathing-space which had been so necessary for reorganization. Twysden continues:

'It is certain that the sitting down before Gloucester gave the Earl of Essex power to recruit himself and with great honour to relieve the town under the Kings nose; to fight him at Newbury; to return himself to London with a high reputation, and, though Aulicus may say he had the worst of the fight, he at least did what he went for; nor did His Majesty ever come to a like opportunity afterwards.

'But to return where I left. The House of Commons, seeing the great success of the King's Armies and expecting him every day at the gates of London, either feared that such as were imprisoned would, upon occasion, be ready to head a party; or, if the King prevailed, they hoped to have the means, by ransoms, exchanges of prisoners, or by some other ways, of bargaining for peace. To this end they ordered, on the 10th August, several prisoners to be committed to certain ships riding in the Thames.'

'By virtue of a warrant this day made by the howse of Commons, these are to will and require you to deliver to those appoynted by the Militia of London, the bodies of Doctor Fairfax, Sr. Roger Twysden, Captayn John Hichwell, Dr. Midleton, Dr. Layfield, to bee by them delivered to George Hawes, Master of the Shippe called the "Prosperous Sarah", now riding in the river of ye Thames, to bee kept in safe custody, as prisoners in ye sayd shippe, by ye sayd George Hawes, untill the pleasure of the howse bee signifyed to ye contrary. And for so doing this shall bee your warrant.

'Wm. Lental, Speaker.

'Dated ye 10th August 1643.'

'When I came to the ship, I observed none but persons of good quality lodged in it; some whom I knew to have been in the King's Army omitted.'

However, Twysden only remained in the *Prosperous Sarah* for a few days, during which he and his fellow prisoners complained so vigorously of being 'stifled with heat and lack of air' in the hold of the ship that they were taken off and Twysden found himself again remitted to 'the Counter'. During the excitement that prevailed in London at this time regarding the King's prospects of success, he was optimistic of being released altogether, and set himself to examine his own legal position together with the causes of his sequestration. He professed himself quite unable to determine the reason why he fell into the category of a 'Notorious Delinquent'. The multitude of the ordinances and the vague interpretations placed upon their clauses rendered any one liable to attachment. What was his fault, and what crime had he committed? He writes to Mr. Dyke, the Sequestrator General for Kent, thus:

'Mr. Dyke, I understand you have warned my tenants not to pay me their rent. If it bee, (as I conceive) in respect of any Ordynance of Parlyament, I desire you will informe me against wch I have offended, Yt I may apply my selfe to a remedy. As for my owne particular, I professe I am ignorant, and am confident, (relying on ye justice of my cause,) that, when ye howse of Commons shall bee at leisure, they will free me with credit. I suppose every man is to have of hys owne to live, tyll hee bee convicted of some enormous offence, and then, in some reasonable measure to bee kept. What my estate is I hear you know as well, if not better, than myself who have beene long absent from any part of it. I have a wife and five children, wth ye care of xx^{ty} that lie upon it; I stand imprisoned in such a place as the charge is not ordynary;—That I am not beefore hand, you can not bee ignorant, by my wanting mony to pay my debts, to wch you are no stranger; I shall entreat you, therefore, not onely out of favour, but justice, to bee a means of remoeving this restreynt from my estate, or at least letting hym know what is ye cause, who for it shall ever

'hold hymself much beehoulding to you,
'ROGER TWYSDEN.

'Counter, Southwark,
    23 October 1643.'

Later to Sir Edward Scot he wrote:

'That I have not been with the King no man doubts; that I never did any disservice to ye Parlyament, is manyfest by my beeing out of ye County now about a year and an half, and so disabled from medling wth ought in it, or elce where; beeing for a good part of yt tyme restreyned of all liberty in prison;— That I have sent ought to Oxford no reasonable man can think, if he know I have wanted for my owne necessary occasions. So yt I assure me I am out of all Orders whatsoever for malignantie or sequestration. And therefore must intreat you, by all our auntient friendship, to bee a means of freeing my rents, wch I am, wth ye more earnestnesse constreyned to presse you to, in respect of ye many inconvenyences ye want of them in this place, where ye charge is not ordinary, makes me undergoe. Sir, I have long experyence of your justice and conscience, and know nothing can make you doe what will not stand wth both; by wch I hope too I shall bee ever dyrected, that am,

'Sr,

'Your humble Servant,

'Counter, Southwark,   'ROGER TWYSDEN.
  30. November 1643.

Dyrected,
    'To my noble friend Sr Edward
    Scot, at hys howse at Scotshall
        in Kent.'

But to neither of these epistles did he get any response.

Being at Southwark, far from Westminster and the environs of the law, he had the utmost difficulty in obtaining legal aid, and was forced to pursue his redresses through his wife and brother-in-law, Yelverton. The latter was now instrumental, through the Chairman of the Committee for Prisoners, Richard Knightly, in procuring his removal to Lambeth, where he was in greater comfort and seclusion and better able to obtain the services of legal advisers. But because of Yelverton's good offices and his aid on behalf of Twysden, he himself was committed to Peterhouse on pretence of having forwarded certain correspondence into France which had been intercepted. He was detained on suspicion for about a month and then released.

Lady Twysden was indefatigable in demanding her husband's rights and inquiring what his fate was to be. All the Committee would tell her was, that if her husband would acknowledge himself 'justly sequestered', they would make an order allowing her a fifth part of his estate, otherwise nothing at all, and would assign no reason for their actions. This was the state of their affairs when she returned, sick with anxiety and illness, to visit her husband in Lambeth on December 21st, 1643.

'About this time, the Committee, seeing God and my Ancestors' care had blest me with good woods, as necessary provision for my house in the country, began to cause such as they interpreted coppice woods to be felled. I was very desirous to have preserved them, such gifts being easily destroyed but with difficulty repaired. But I failed in my hopes and in this sad condition I stood at the conclusion of the year 1643. My estate in a posture of being ruined by the Kentish Committee, nothing allowed me to live on and myself in a prison. In this extremity I caused a petition to be delivered to the Lords and Commons for Sequestration at Westminster, who, upon the 16th February, 1644 thought fit and ordered that—"It be referred to the Committee for Sequestrations in ye County of Kent, to certify ye grounds and causes of ye Sequestration of ye sayd Sr. Roger Twysden to this Committee; and, in ye mean tyme, to forbear the cutting downe or spoyle of any Tymber Trees, or other woods, wth in ye scite, or for ye defence of any hys Mansion howses.   JOHN WYLDE." '

The Committee of Kent, however, in no wise restrained their persecution of him nor abated their timber-cutting activities at Roydon. They replied by setting out their views of the causes of Sir Roger's sequestration as follows:

'20 Febr. 1644.

'The Certificate from ye Committee of Kent, towching ye Sequestration of Sr. Roger Twysden's Estate.

'For ye causes of Sequestration, wee hope the Parlyament will not put such a trust by their Ordinances to men yt will sequester wth out cause. And, allthough it may very well happen, yt in some cases, wee can not carry the Sequestration and cause in mynd, to give a speedy accoumpt thereof; yet, in this case of Sr Roger Twysden's, wee could not expect now to be called to an accoumpt, there beeing so many concurrent causes even knowne to all ye Parlyament. First, he stood committed about the Petition, formed and framed by hym self and Sr Edward Dering, wch hath beene ye principall (if not the onely) cause of all ye rebellion in Kent. Upon hys releas by band not to come in to Kent wth out leave, after his long obscuring, was taken by ye Committees flying into France, in a false disguise, wth a false passe, and under a false name, denying hymself and byrth, so far as to abuse hymself to bee a serving man to a stranger and a Papist.

'Besides all this, he hath beene refractory to all proceedings of Parlyament; not onely in hymself, but in anymating hys neighbourhood, in so much, there was scarse one neere hym not in ye rebellion; Hys holding correspondence by letters intercepted, both to Priests in hys own County, and strangers abroad, of ille consequence; If there were no other witnesse, his absenting hymself is, by ye Ordinance, one of those characters for Sequestration; If all this together bee not sufficient to sequester hym who had sequestered hymself from hys name, hys famyly, hys estate, and even from hymself, untill, by the pulling of hys disguise, he beegan to call hymself to remembrance, wee confesse wee understand not how to proceede upon yt Ordinance; but shall bee very tender heereafter, when such an accoumpt is required, for so notorious a Delinquent; of

'JOHN WILD. (Wylde)
'Knowle, this 20th of February 1643/4.'

Twysden was filled with indignation upon receiving this indictment—for such it was—and at once conceived it to have been written by the order of Sir Anthony Weldon, Chairman of the Committee, attempting to abuse his unfortunate situation to pay off some old family scores, in which he was aided and abetted by his colleague, Sir John Sedley. The lattter, as we have seen, bore an implacable hatred against Twysden, and had been heard to swear that 'Ere he had done, he would not leave a Twysden worth a groat in Kent'.

In the hands of these vindictive gentlemen of the Parliament we can easily appreciate Twysden's plight. Having him now completely in their power, it was not likely they would fail to find sufficient excuse for keeping him in safe custody for an indefinite period. Nevertheless, Twysden continued to worry them almost daily with voluminous letters and questionnaires, together with weekly petitions to both houses and to any one of his influential friends whom he could conceive might be of help. So much did he belabour them with his protestations that they were forced, for lack of fresh arguments, to refuse any longer to discuss the affairs of his estate. The subsequent order issued from Knole was a masterpiece of muddle and contradiction.

'By ye Order dated ye 14 June, 1644.

'Whereas ye Committee of Lords and Commons for Sequestrations have ordered that there should bee a respit of felling or carrying-away any woods of Sr. Roger Twysden, until ye day of hearing appoynted by the last Order; Upon Complaynt made to this Committee, and on the beehalf of such as have contracted for woods of Sr. Roger Twysden's, whch were felled and sold beefore the last Order, Wee are of opinion that the sayd order does not extend anyways to ye prejudice of any such former contracts; but that ye sayd parties may lawfully take and carry away such woods so bargained or contracted for, and that such wood as was cut beefore ye last Order, may bee sold.

'Knoll, ye 19 June, 1644.'

In Twysden's inimitable words it is thus described:

'I shall not need here to set down who were the subscribers of this Order: It shall suffice to say it was done by seven; three of whom, I am persuaded, did not in their heart approve it, but carried with the hurry, might not refuse. The 19th June was past felling for this year,—My Lady Day's rents they had already received,—All woods contracted for might be carried away!—All felled, not yet exposed to sale, might be sold!—thus, following the example of their Masters the House of Commons, they did, by their viperine glosses, wipe me of receiving any benefit by the former order; and when my wife complained above, the only answer she received was "The Committee of Kent would do what they would do".' [The words of Pontius Pilate, driven into a corner, inevitably occur to mind.]

It was, however, beginning reluctantly to dawn upon Twysden that his implication in the issue of the Petition of Kent was the real reason for his persecution—as it undoubtedly was. On the 21st August he was remanded to Goldsmiths' Hall for the first time to be examined by the Officers of Treasury for Sequestration. Being brought into the 'Painted Chamber' before a Committee of Lords and Commons sitting, he was confronted with 'all persons I think I had ever spoken to about that Petition, with Mr. Lambert Godfrey as Sequestrator General of Kent. Mr. James spake very little but could not deny I had recommended it unto him—Sir John Rivers,[1] that he knew I was for it because I had told him he had not the wit to understand it.' 'Sir John Sedley having now opportunity of shewing his affection to me, urged with much vehemence that I was with him when it was considered at Maidstone. To which the Chairman replied, "Why did you not come away then? Did he shut the door upon you?" At which having stood as though a little stunned by the question, pulling himself together and recollecting, he answered, "Yes, he did and would not let me out," ' the correctness of which statement Twysden had little difficulty in disproving. He also no doubt availed himself of the opportunity of exercising some of his personal feelings against his hated rival and sworn enemy.

Whether or not the weight of evidence was against him, it was now clear beyond doubt that the ostensible reason for Twysden's persecution was his complicity in the petition. It is put on record in an order emanating from the Kent Committee on August 23rd, 1644, confirming that 'The estate of the said Sir Roger Twysden do continue under Sequestration, and that the Committee of Sequestration in Kent do proceed in the execution of the said

[1] Of Chafford in Penshurst; property alienated and mansion since pulled down.

Order, anything to the contrary notwithstanding.' And in the handwriting of the officer in authority (Richard Vaughan), the grounds for sequestration are noted, viz. 'For associating in ye Kentish Petition' (*signed* Rd. Vaughan).

'Here you see me now stript of all whatsoever but a prison; yet the crime not so notorious but it did admit of a long and serious debate. No cause alleged; no affirmation of the particular thing I was charged with being within the Ordinance of Sequestration, or what that was. Only the Clerk in the margin from memory had made an entry as though an intention to petition Parliament was to be interpreted as actually associating against the Parliament; which makes me see how ill it is to have anything penal left to the will of a Judge especially a Committee. And this our ancestors have in former times had experience of in days when the House of Commons endeavoured to save men's estates; not, as now, to ruin them.'

'I dare say whatsoever was or could be said, my Estate must be exposed to the fury of the Kentish Committee; Had I been as innocent as Abel, or as guilty as Judas, all one.'

CHAPTER IX

SIR ROGER TWYSDEN AND THE CIVIL WAR
PART III

Twysden's diary has, for the sake of convenience, been divided into three parts. The last of these is an account of the abuses of his estate by the Parliament; of the efforts of himself and Lady Twysden to obtain some redress; of his relations and friends to obtain his release, and of their endeavours on his behalf to resist the heavy payments at which he was assessed for the compounding of his property. The late summer of 1644 found him in reasonably comfortable confinement at Lambeth, where he continued throughout the following year, without any satisfaction, until he at last gained his freedom in February 1646, though by no means a final settlement regarding his estate.

The fortunes of the parties in the Civil War had undergone considerable change, and the turn of the tide had come when the Royalists had received their first real reverse at Marston Moor in July 1644. The disintegration of their command grew with the King's lack of purpose, while on the other hand the breathing space afforded to the Parliament by his indecision was turned to the fullest advantage. The Roundhead leadership underwent thorough reorganization and a change for the better. A regular army was trained and supported with serviceable material and unfailing pay.

One of the heaviest drawbacks with which the King and his brilliant nephew Prince Rupert had to contend was lack of money. Another was the difficulty of getting the local supporters who rallied to the Royal Standard to venture far from their own homes or outside their counties. The disposition of the King's forces was so scattered that those who joined his armies were in constant fear of being cut off from their homes, leaving their families unprotected against the enemy behind them. Rupert's untiring energy was used up in efforts constantly necessary for raising fresh troops. His judgement was undermined by the King's lack of confidence in him, and his courage was sapped by those around the King's person who were hostile to him. A man whose greatest assets as a leader were speed, brilliance, and the ruthless pursuit of the main object, Rupert stood little chance among the vain and self-seeking courtiers who composed the majority of the King's War Council and personal bodyguard. His regular army of fighting cavalry was far too small for a good general to risk the desperate encounters he was forced to launch owing to the ill timing of actions in the later stages of the war. Their outcome was less sure of success and the attendant risk was accordingly much greater.

Twysden, within the compass of his walls at Lambeth, shows no sign of partisanship at this time. Only now and then in his diary is there any hint or expression which gives a clue to his real sympathies, and even these are carefully hedged. He could hardly have suffered worse things had he been openly taking an active part, but so great was his sense of injustice that he was more busily engaged in airing his own grievances than discoursing on the rights and wrongs of the constitutional issues at stake. He felt certain that both sides would come to terms. Neither Covenanters nor Parliamentarians yet visualized the extreme measures which ultimately were to be taken, and occasions were constantly arising when one side or other desired to treat for peace.

In the late summer of 1643, such had been the successes of the King's generals, Rupert at Bristol, Hopton in the west country, and the Duke of Newcastle in the north, that a motion in the House of Commons to sue for peace had only been defeated by seven votes. Each opportunity missed meant not only the prolongation of the struggle but the increase of its bitterness. Small wonder that the

Parliament had little time or inclination to give a fair hearing to delinquents and those suspected of malignancy. Nor were they likely to loosen a hold once gained on persons who bore the faintest suspicion of partiality to the Royalist cause, least of all upon the estates and possessions of such persons, which, if the struggle was to be long drawn out, would count for so much in the provision of money—that all decisive factor in the end.

It is not surprising that Twysden and his likes, in spite of their most justifiable complaints, got little in the way of fair treatment and even less of sympathy, nor that their friends and counsel refused to risk their reputations by giving whole-hearted support to their cause. Isabella, Lady Twysden, herself left no stone unturned. She sought out every one of their friends who might have had any influence, in the endeavour to persuade them to exercise it on her husband's behalf. With such an able and devoted agent working for him, Twysden had to remain as satisfied as his circumstances permitted, and apart from directing operations from his prison, there was nothing else that he could do to further the interests of his estate. He consoled himself by spending the time in pursuit of his studies and writings. Much of his literary work, as we have already observed, was completed during this period of otherwise enforced idleness.

But to return to Roydon, we must examine the serious effects which the misfortunes of its master were having upon the house and estate. The confusion caused by the various authorities endeavouring to collect the rents brought much discomfort to his tenants, who never were assured of their proper discharge and never knew whether the dues were going to be demanded more than once. The orders and counter-orders relative to the cutting of timber—the most valuable asset on the estate—were another disadvantage which a hitherto soundly administered property could not be expected indefinitely to withstand.

In addition to this, the house was constantly searched

under warrant; the servants were questioned and abused, and inventories were taken which placed the most fantastic values upon the contents with a view to the unfortunate owner being forced to make a heavy composition later for his own possessions.

Lady Twysden spent her time between Roydon, Lambeth, and Maidstone, attending there at the summons of the local committee. She was ill with worry over her husband's plight and was expecting confinement at an early date for the birth of what was to be their youngest son Charles. In spite of her condition she rode constantly to and fro between Maidstone and Roydon to appear before her inquisitors, at whose hands she suffered the greatest insult and indignity. Twysden's fortunes were at a low ebb. Roydon was derelict and his family were scattered. His elder children were in France, whither he had sent them with a reliable friend and tutor, Dr. Hamnet Ward. His London house in Redcross Street had long since been ransacked and the contents assessed at a fine of four hundred pounds. Even his house at Chelmington in Great Chart had been visited, and although there was little of value there, the Parliament agents took everything there was. His diary at this juncture is one continual complaint of injustice done to him through the maladministration of his lands and the cutting of his precious timber at Roydon.

'Being in prison, having no good opinion of any good could come to me, some friends of mine, nothing satisfied with the injustice of the former sentence (of sequestration), and desiring to preserve my estate from waste and utter ruin, intended to have made trial whether they could have got me tenant to it. (As my Lady Finch of Fordich was of her husband Sir George Sonds.)'[1]

The Committee of Kent, having gained intelligence of

---

[1] Sir George Sondes was of Lees Court, near Faversham. He was imprisoned several years, his house plundered more than once and his estates sequestered. He was the father of George and Freeman Sondes, whose unhappy story is too well known to need repetition here. At the Restoration he was created Earl of Faversham and Viscount Sondes. (*Arch. Cant.*, vol. ii, pp. 86–9, and Appendix I.)

Twysden's purpose, immediately wrote this letter to the Parliament:

'My Lords and gentlemen, understanding of some endeavors of Sr. Roger Twysden, or some friends of hys, to procure an Order from your hon^ble Committee, to become tenants to his estate, wee thought ourselves to represent unto you the mischiefs which are like to ensue upon such kind of dimises.

'i.   It admits or creates a disposing power in ye Delinquent, wch can not but prejudice ye Parlyament, both in poynt of interest and honor.

'ij.   It exposeth such tenants as have beene active for the Parlyament, or conformable to it in due payment of their rents, to ye revenge and spleene of their old malignant Landlord; eyther by beeing turned out of their ferms, or otherwise discountenanced or discouraged.

'iij.   It gives a Latitude, eyther to ye Delinquent, or to hys intrusted friend, to ingratiate to hym a disaffected party, by these dependencies upon hym and hys tenants. At least wise, it obligeth the fermors (who are ye strength of ye County) to a condition of neutralyty, through hope or fear of their malignant Landlord's frowne or favour; and, by consequence, lays a foundation of disservice to ye Parlyament, and insecuryty to ye Parlyament.

(Signed) R. VAUGHAN—Knoll, 4 Sept. 1644.'

'I had a very great desire to have saved my seat from utter defacing; and my woods lying about my house I did labour to have allotted as my wife's fifth part. Out of these hopes she petitioned, the 6th September 1644, Mr. Browne (who truly I take in his own nature to be a just man) sitting in the Chair. Upon her desire of having the lands about my mansion house included in her fifth part, when some question was made of it, "Yes, yes," said he, "let her have them, she hath had measure hard enough".'

So in the end she obtained an order, not peremptory, but recommendatory, to the Committee of Kent upon the same day, as follows:

'Upon the complaint of Dame Isabella Twysden, wife of Sir Roger Twysden, Baronet, it is thought fit and ordered, that the Committee of Kent do allow the said Lady a fifth part of her

husband's estate, according to the Ordinance; and it is recommended to the said Committee to let the said Lady have her
Mansion House, and the lands adjoining, in case her fifth part
amount to so much.' 'Sam Browne.'

'In pursuit of this Order, my wife, now great with child and
a very weak body, thought fit to attend the Committee of Kent
for her fifth part. So down she went on September 17th, with
her Order of the sixth to them at Knole. When she appeared
before them, Sir Anthony Weldon, then in the Chair, told her
he heard she was come into the Country, and that he wondered
how she durst. . . .

'There was present Sir Edward Monyngs,[1] who, as he was a
near kinsman of mine and an honest gentleman, so he showed
himself always a worthy friend to her and me; and by his means
Mr. Oxenden also, to whom I may add Mr. James and Sir
Nicholas Miller, that I daresay desired not to have done mischief in general to any man, nor to me in particular, could they
have prevailed. But the leading men were here now the
violent.'

Being caused to stand, as she was through the whole of
her examination by the committee, Lady Twysden replied
that she came to her own house. Weldon told her
peremptorily it was not her own but the State's. She then
presented them with her Order (which they took little
notice of) and desired that she might become the tenant
of her husband's estate, which was absolutely refused.
They pressed her hard for particulars of it, which she told
them they knew better than herself since the committee
had received the rents for a year and a half. Much had
been altered in the meantime while they had had the disposing of it, so she excused herself from giving the
required particulars, which at the time she protested she
was quite unable to do. The chairman told her that as
soon as ever Michaelmas was past they would have all the
rents and she nothing of them. Another member added

[1] Monins—Jane Twysden. Jane was the youngest daughter of Roger Twysden and sister to Sir William the 1st Baronet. She was therefore an aunt of Sir
Roger. She married Sir William Monins of Waldershare, Bt., who died in
1643. Their son, Edward, succeeded to the baronetcy of Waldershare and was
first cousin to Sir Roger Twysden. (*Arch. Cant.*, vol. iv, and Twysden Pedigree.)

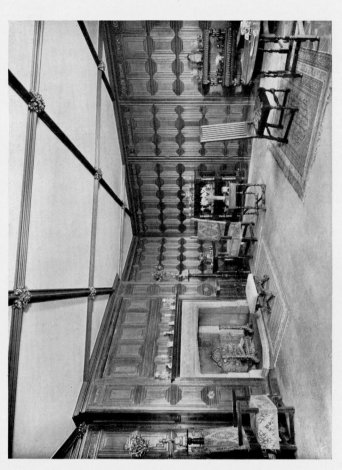

THE GREAT PARLOUR IN LADY TWYSDEN'S TIME

Decorative moulded panelling of the Jacobean period and carved stone fireplace. The Roydon motto appears as a frieze

that if she did not bring in a rent roll before Michaelmas she would find it worse afterwards. Having no alternative but to submit to this treatment, she returned to her husband at Lambeth with nothing gained. In the following November she braved the committee again, attending before them at the house of Sir Peter Ricault at Aylesford,[1] but the result was little better, the only outcome being that they sent their agents, including one Walter Brooke of Yalding, to view the farm and lands in East Peckham in the occupation of George Stone for the purpose of certifying the number of acres, the yearly value, and the quantity of woods, and their condition, lying within that part of which Lady Twysden was claiming her portion, or fifth part of the estate; return thereof to be made within ten days. But the following day they received information that a quantity of *valuable goods*[2] lay undiscovered at Roydon, and in consequence ordered that stay be made of Lady Twysden's claim to a fifth part until discovery of the goods in the House be made.

[1] This was the Friars, Aylesford, afterwards the property of the Earl of Aylesford. Sir Peter had suffered the sequestration of his estates for his attachment to the royal cause. He himself was one of the persons excepted in the propositions of the Lords and Commons for a safe and well-grounded peace in July 1646, forwarded to Charles at Newcastle. He had ten children, the youngest of whom was the eminent Sir Paul Ricault, celebrated as an historical writer as well as a diplomat and statesman.

[2] The following memorandum from Sir Roger's private diary is a laughable comment upon Sir Anthony Weldon's demand. It is an inventory of these *spolia opima* supposed to be hidden at Roydon Hall:

'Things caryed out of my house in East Peckham, by ye Troopers, on Wensday ye of April, 1643.

'A saddle.

'2 or 3 byts, gyrts, snaffles, styrrops, and all of y^t kind they met with.

'Nurse her lased handkerchiefe.

'Wm. Sparks' shirts, 3 bands, 4s. 8d. in money, a boxe in sylver out of my wive's closet.

'Captayn Vaughan's* two handed sword.

'A glove of male.

'A booke and a payr of compasses.

'A payr of Pystol cases, a combe, and a book or two of Ward's (Hamnet Ward).

'A little dagger, two belts, and gyrdles.

'2 little bookes of waxe candles.'

(*Arch. Cant.* Ed.)

---

* Vaughan was the second husband of Twysden's great-grandmother Elizabeth Roydon. See Chapter IV.

'And here to speak a word of my goods, which they had been here several times to search after, the best of which I had transported beyond seas and were there for the most part lost; the others I had committed to those I knew faithful and out of their power. Yet Sir Anthony Weldon told my wife the goods were of great value, worth ten thousand pounds, and sent Mr. Wolf divers times with soldiers to search for them, who, finding nothing but what the children lay on or employed in their necessary use, made return that truly there was not any. At this Sir Anthony chafed; told Wolf he would turn him out of his place.'

Wolf protested that he was not the only one that had made the search but that there were thirty soldiers with him who could testify that there was nothing to be taken away.

Twysden, commenting upon the waste of time and labour, not to say the inconvenience and insult suffered by his wife through all these orders and examinations, says:

'Yet I think not unfit to tell the Reader what I have heard, and seems to me not improbable. That some of them (the Committee) having carried themselves so desperately to my ruin, yet finding, by relation, a good quantity of wood to be still standing, so as I might come to live at my House again, they resolved to have it cut down, that by so doing it might be made absolutely unserviceable for the future. . . . The Reader may believe what pleaseth him.'

'My dear wife, great with child, and now ready to lie in, went down into Kent on the 8th of February (1645). And though she rode all the way on horseback behind George Stone, yet God so enabled her, a weak body, she had no hurt. To Him therefore be the praise, for that and all His other goodness to me and her, for ever and ever, Amen. But whether it was owing to her many journeys on my errands, an unhappy midwife, or what else, I know not, she had a very ill time after her being delivered; and indeed never recovered her former strength during all her life, in so much as she returned not to me again till the 23rd of May following.'

On the 11th March, 1645, Twysden was again brought from Lambeth to Goldsmiths' Hall, where he was informed that a fine of £3,000 had been levied upon his estate. The chairman, Mr. John Ash, stated formally, 'We sit here to oppress no man. For my part I think this gentleman has had very hard measure; but we can do him no good, other than give him time for payment.' Twysden, dumbfounded and shocked at this sum, asked them if they could tell him how to obtain redress, to which the answer was by petition to the House, which they as a body were not constituted to receive or to put forward.

'Being out of prison, I went to my brother Yelverton to speak to him a word about this fine. He assured me that if I would acknowledge myself a Delinquent (which I could not bring myself to do) it would be mitigated. I desired it might have a full hearing in the House and then I might know if I was at fault and submit myself if they concluded me to be so. But this was not to be expected as they were so full of business, especially if the case were such, the party had hope of being freed of Sequestration.

'Now alone (returned to Lambeth) and my wife gone from me, I began to consider the power and privileges of the two Houses, as they stood apart and did not join with the King; especially of the House of Commons and how far they might legally demand obedience from the subject; whether they had any privilege or right to govern the nation, otherwise than by the known laws of the land. To which purpose, being helped with some good books from my noble friend Sir Simonds D'ieux; from which, joining with them my own collections, I gathered a good quantity of notes and am resolved here to set them down as they may perhaps be useful to some who come after me.'

It has been previously mentioned that when Twysden was restricted to the boundaries of London while on bail after his first apprehension in 1642, he passed much of the time searching among the Records at the Tower. 'The elasticity of a powerful mind ever increases with the pressure imposed upon it.' So it was with him. Indeed, it is probable that had this good man not suffered the persecution that he did, we might never have possessed those carefully composed and learned treatises upon the

Constitution of England that were handed down as literary masterpieces of his time.

'This year (1645) my dear wife looking after my business, I had the liberty of following my studies and finding human nature can never be absolutely idle, put out the Laws of Henry I, compared with the red book in the Exchequer never before printed, and joined them with the Saxon Laws set out by Mr. Lambert in 1568 and with those of the Conqueror, published by Mr. Selden. And so passed them to the Press with a preface of my own—which is the first time I ever appeared in print.'

The deciphering and symposium of these tracts alone might well have been considered a veritable life's work.

Meanwhile, in regard to the timber on the Roydon estate, the committee were busy issuing their contradictory orders. A Parliament commission presided over by John Wylde respecting the supply of fuel for the Cities of London and Westminster ordered a stay of felling any further woods at Roydon, Lady Twysden to have as her portion any part of the said woods already felled after the order became effective.

'You may think by this, the Committee at Westminster had an intent to have done me some right after that severe sentence; but the Committee of Kent was resolute. I must have neither favour nor justice, or as a gentleman from them told me, I should never be unsequestered without applying myself to them, which as yet I could not be persuaded to do; it being certain I must first have taken the Covenant and joined with them in all their injustice, at least so far as not to have shown a dislike of their actions. But with that Order my dear wife went down into Kent, where I will leave her a while and look back touching the felling of these woods.

'In February 1644 they first began with three woods of mine: Prior's Broome (by some called Brown's Wood because one Browne had sometime bought it of my father when felled) and the Shetes. A second named Motewood, both in Nettlestead. A third Offam, or Oven's Wood, in Wateringbury, neither fully twenty years' growth, in which they used me so barbarously that, my wife not having her fifth part assigned, they forced the tenant who provided for my house and children to pay for the wood himself and this in spite of their taking every farthing they could any way come by. But then they left Stokenbury Wood unfelled, being oak of far the greatest growth and more fit to be cut and which I myself was in process of doing before I came into trouble; so this Stokenbury Wood was left uncut all 1644. Supposing the timber on account of its name to grow out of old *stocks* or upon some information, I know not what, came to this resolution; that woods of oak, though never so great, yet growing not clear out of the ground, was not to be reputed timber. And this I hold every whit as unjust as the sentence of Sequestration, as contrary to all experience, that ever reputed of good use such, for building and other things about husbandry, and contrary to the Kentish proverb:

> 'The Oak that grows on the Father's head
> Is as good Timber as ever was bred.'

'But I resolved to drive the nail as far as it would go, so sent down to have a true certificate rendered to me of the nature of Stokenbury, such as, if need were, would be sworn to. Upon which I had shortly after this return, in effect, from four persons well experienced in such affairs: That Stokenbury Wood was above 30 years growth—that a part of it, which was felled some five years since was then employed for Rails, Laths, Ploughs, Rafter and other necessaries about building: that what was now remaining was more fit for those or the like uses than that which had already been cut; that when it was heretofore felled by my father, being about the growth it now is, it was so used: that they did conceive that being oak of 30 years standing it ought to be reputed Timber; that to be felled and not so employed would be a loss to the parts adjacent; that it was about half a mile from my Mansion House, and those felled the year before even nearer, to the great defacement thereof.

'Having this information, and likewise that they had felled a thousand young straight timber trees, 20, 30 and 40 foot long, without even a bough, tall and coming clear and free of themselves, I got my noble friend Sir Simonds D'ieux (a person never wearied of doing courtesies) to move the Committee at Westminster, suggesting they had cut down 500 Timber trees and denied my wife her fifth part of the said woods.'

In the summer of 1645, when Twysden was driven nearly to distraction by the helplessness of his plight, his brother-in-law Sir Christopher and Lady Yelverton came down to stay at Roydon, deeming it unwise by reason of the King's Garrison at Banbury to remain at their own home, Easton Maudit, in Northamptonshire. On arrival they were horrified at the mutilation of the woods and the general dilapidation of the estate and were determined to rally Twysden to further efforts to redeem himself from the hardships under which he suffered. Yelverton was accordingly stimulated into action on Twysden's behalf and together with his cousin Richard Browne visited him in Lambeth to discuss his affairs, and persuaded him to deliver a petition;

'which was a huge difficulty to get into the house of Commons, as I myself waited two years afterwards to get it done. For such was the justice of that house and their Committee, that if one committed by them lay under an oppression they could not colourably deny the relieving of him; then, by the greatness of public affairs, they would not be at leisure to hear him. . . . God of his mercy deliver the nation from such like tyrannical oppression for the future! Let him that had no feeling of it pray he never may and he shall die happy! But I return to my brother (in law) Yelverton, whom I left engaged to get my petition into the House of Commons.'

In the following autumn the parties were successful in framing and forwarding this petition, which on December 9th, 1645, came before the House:

'The humble petition of Sir Roger Twysden, now prisoner at Lambeth, was this day read and it is therefore ordered that he be forthwith bailed. And it is referred to the Committee of Lords and Commons for sequestration to report the state of the case concerning Sir Roger Twysden to the House, that they may thereupon take such order therein, as they shall think fit.

'Hen. Elsyng, Cler. Parl.—D. Com'.

'The next day my sister, Lady Yelverton herself, good soul, brought it me. And though it were not much, yet truly was more than I expected.'

In spite of this order, Twysden could not immediately
get out of Lambeth. For now he had to come to a reckon-
ing with his keeper, one Dr. Alexander Leighton, a Scots-
man, and an earnest Presbyterian, who had not many
years before been censured in the Star Chamber for a book
entitled *Zion's Plea against the Prelacy*. The worthy doctor,
finding himself in the fortunate position of being able to
make an excellent profit out of the misfortunes of wealthy
'malignants', was not slow in drawing up his own set of
rules regarding the terms and conditions of their imprisonment, together with a scale of payments suitable to their
circumstances. As Twysden says, 'Since my coming into
that House I had paid him above £15 for bare walls, three
pair of stairs high, being the lodging of one only person
of the many who belonged to the Archbishop.' Dr.
Leighton, no doubt in his anxiety to lose no opportunity
of enriching the Archbishop's coffers, lost few of enriching himself, for, as our friend declares, 'although no ill-
dispositioned person, he was one who loved the Pres-
bytery and loved money'.

'And now I return to my prison out of which I was freed the
20th February 1646 having remained there two years all but
two days; from thence I went to a lodging in Westminster, a
Mr. Austin's in St. Anne Street, where I abode two years more,
during all of which time I was few mornings (unless when fear
of sickness drove me into the country) from the Parliament
door. Into the hands of all my friends I put Petitions to the
House, that they appoint a day to see their order of December
9th 1645 put into execution. Meeting Mr. John Selden[1] one
day, he spoke to me of my sequestration and I to him of this
order. He ingenuously told me I would never get off but by
compounding at Goldsmiths' Hall. Neither by friends, favour
nor money could I get it heard.

'I went to Mr. Ash, the Chairman at Goldsmiths' Hall, who
told me truly and honestly that they could not compound with
me in the ordinary way according to the value of my estate,
because everything laid against me was prior to the 20th May

[1] This was the learned John Selden, who assisted Sir Roger Twysden in the
publication of the *Decem Scriptores*, and with whom he always maintained close
intimacy and friendship. (*Arch. Cant.*)

1642, the time the war began. If I would pay £3,000 I might be received by them. And here is a strange matter. I was not so notorious a Delinquent, but whether I was within the order or not was a question. But such as fought against the Parliament might, and did, come off much better and at far easier rates than I, who never was out of the Parliament's quarters.

'So dangerous is it to trust a multitude with the administration of Justice, whose severity usually increases with their prosperity. If I did compound I must needs take the Scottish Covenant. Thus I stood in expectation until after the King's death, seeing my estate wither away little by little, yet without power to help it.'

Twysden did not see his way to taking the Scots Oath, unless it was upon his own terms and with his own reservations. In March 1649 the Parliament had made an absolute conquest. The King was dead and the nation was subdued and sullen under the shock of this extremity. Twysden with redoubled energy set himself to obtain the release of his estates, realizing that, where justice did not exist, he had best strive to save his title and something from the wreck, even though the demands laid upon him should prove the veriest extortion.

Composition became a matter of making the best bargain under the circumstances and obtaining as large a discount as possible for immediate payment. There were those who 'admitted to pay a full sixth of the true value of their estates, half of it down, the other half three months after'. If anything was discovered of a greater value than had been declared by the party himself it was to be forfeited. So also were the estates of those who neglected to compound. No allowances were made for dependants. Those whose estates were still unnegotiated by March 21st, 1649, but who subsequently completed their composition within the limited number of days specified, were to be exempt from paying the levy of 20 per cent. upon them:

'Accordingly I went again to Goldsmiths' Hall and in full Committee presented my Petition. The Clerk found I had been set at £3000 by the House, and without paying that there was no hope of compounding, so away I was forced: In this encounter I observed no man more sharp than Sir Arthur Haselrig,[1] whereupon I went to him and by means of a very noble gentleman, one Mr. George Fenwick, spoke with him. Having informed him of my case I found him much other than I apprehended, for he not only assisted me in drawing up a Petition to the House but advised me to get young Sir Henry Vane[2] to deliver it. Old Sir Henry Vane, and young, spoke earnestly for me. So did many more. Sir Lislebon Long, now Knighted and Recorder of London, also solicited his friends on my behalf. I may not forget a gentleman of whom I received so signal a favour.

'The Truth is, Sir Anthony Weldon now dead, and Sir John Sedley's power, by his own carriage (behaviour), taken away; my woods, the great eye-sore, destroyed, I found the Committee of Kent not so eager against me and my address more facile to the Parliament. But what was to be done was the question. Sir Arthur Haselrig (truly I am persuaded, having experience of the delays of that House, out of an intent to do me good) pitched upon this: that I should compound at a tenth, that is two years' revenue of my Estate and not above.'

This was easily assented to and an order made thereupon, May 19th, 1649, 'That Sir Roger Twysden, notwithstanding the fine imposed upon him by a former vote at this House, be referred to the Committee at Goldsmiths' Hall, to compound at a tenth, and not above.'

Twysden, after due consideration and consultation with his friends and counsel, decided 'to make an end of a tedious business and embrace it'. His ultimate fine was fixed at £1,340, half to be paid within fourteen days and the remainder six weeks afterwards. He finally obtained his discharge in January 1650 and returned to Roydon to find it 'miserably torn and ransacked by these men'.

If we have dwelt unduly long over this interesting diary it is through anxiety not to omit any of the writer's

---

[1] Member for Leicestershire, one of the most violent of the Regicides, and the first designer of the Abolition Bill. It was he who, with Oliver Cromwell and Sir Henry Vane, put this Bill into Sir Edward Dering's hands and inveigled him into presenting that odious measure to the House. (*Arch. Cant.* Ed.)

[2] Note, p. 102.

true feelings towards the times. The subject brings to bear many illuminating and forceful points of view upon the overwhelming troubles that taxed the honest and scrupulous landed proprietor in the Civil War, and conveys a wealth of sentiment and reflection which, though weighted with many complaints, must claim to have been expressed moderately and with courageous endurance. Furthermore Twysden, in relating his own experience, is at the same time describing the lot of hundreds of fellow sufferers of his own class throughout the kingdom, who no doubt endured equally hard treatment. It may even be that by his knowledge and persistence he got off more lightly than many other less accomplished men, and some less fortunate than himself, who barely escaped losing their lives through taking part in the struggle.

The diary ends upon a pious and meditative note, showing clearly that the writer is worn out and resigned. The editor of the manuscript comments upon the fact that there is a considerable amount of confusion and erasion at the end, no doubt because of an endeavour at a later date to reconcile the closing words to the existing state of affairs. The word 'King' has been inserted in front of 'Protector', probably after, and as a result of, the Restoration. Thus it concludes:

'And here, having shewd how I fell into these troubles, how miserably I was tortured under them, and how God in his good time, in part delivered me out of them, there remains that I render Him all humble and hearty thanks for this gracious assistance to me and mine during the continuance of them: and in the end, by an unexpected hand, freeing this nation of their heavy task-masters, that men may live more quietly and enjoy with more freedom their own houses and thoughts.

'God of His mercy grant that for the future there may never be seen a perpetuity added to the two Houses of Parliament, nor Committees to manage the justice of the Kingdom and sit as judges of men's liberties, estates and fortunes—which, as things now stand, is a thing rather to be prayed for than expected. Neither can I find any way how it can be; but must remit all to the only wise God, who of His infinite goodness, and pity of the miseries of this distracted nation, may be pleased to find some means of restoring every one to their rights and the Law to its vigour by a just *King Protector* of it; without which I shall never look for a lasting Peace. Thus it is this 11th of December 1657, and so to see it shall ever be the prayer of Roger Twysden.'

CHAPTER X

THE EIGHTEENTH CENTURY

AFTER the Restoration Roydon ceased to be affected by national events, and William Twysden set himself to repair the damage done in the time of his illustrious father. It is probable that some restitution was made for the ravages upon his property, but the hewn timber could not be replaced, nor could any reparation make the oaks grow faster. He did a great deal to the house itself and actually completed the building, decorating the porch in the Italian style which Wren himself was busy interpreting at the time. To the east of the house he made a beautiful garden which he enclosed with a wall.[1] The heavy burden which these additions imposed upon his already impoverished fortune, as a result of the depredations of the Civil War, were not made good by his son Thomas, the eldest survivor of nine sons, who succeeded him in 1697 when only 21 years old.

In 1710 Thomas married Catherine Withers, reputed to have been the mistress of Sir Thomas Culpepper of Aylesford, and had two daughters, the second of whom was born six months after his death, which occurred in 1712. He was succeeded by his younger brother William, who in 1706 had married his second cousin Jane, granddaughter of Sir Thomas Twisden of Bradbourne, thus reuniting the two branches of the family.

It is not surprising that the eighteenth century, besides being a less eventful one for Roydon, witnessed the decline of the Twysdens, nor that Roydon, like many other estates of its size in England, failed to escape the hardships through which agriculture was passing during the first half of the century.

At this conjuncture it is proposed to submerge the chronicles of the succeeding Twysdens in the wider sphere

[1] See chapter on 'Architecture'.

of the political and social history of the time, to show the tendencies which were affecting so profoundly the fortunes of the country squire throughout England and the vast changes which were brought about by the Industrial Revolution with its concurrent upheaval of the farming community.

We shall see how the eventual disposal of Roydon by the descendant of an old Royalist family to a successful merchant-prince was but the natural outcome of the century's development and a marked tendency of the period. As the one declined, the other arose and prospered. In order, therefore, to link up the seventeenth and nineteenth centuries in the story of Roydon it will be necessary to examine briefly the great political and social events that occurred during the intervening hundred years. No portrait would be adequate if it failed to illustrate the fundamental changes that took place between the beginning and end of the eighteenth century in the character and habits of the people, and the physical alterations in the face of the countryside in which they lived.

The England of George the Fourth could be said to bear only a faint resemblance by comparison to the England of Queen Anne. Within this relatively short space of time, all its Tudor likeness had disappeared—a likeness, familiar to Shakespeare, that subsisted for nearly three hundred years. There came into being the country of Byron and Shelley, of Disraeli and Gladstone.

The arrival of the Princes of Hanover is commonly supposed to have opened up a new chapter in English history. But for a long time afterwards there remained a Jacobite enthusiasm which was barely suppressed, and every now and then came to the surface under the reign of the first two Georges. The almost successful venture of 1715 to re-establish upon the throne the 'True and Rightful King', and the attempt thirty years later to install his son, clearly indicated that throughout this time a strong element of Stuart reaction was present, and that the return of either Old or Young Pretender would probably have been hailed with almost as much jubilation as was that of Charles II at the Restoration. Enthusiasm and devotion to the Stuarts were in ample evidence. Even the Tory party itself fell into disrepute because of its suspected proclivities towards their cause. But, as ever, it was attended by that lack of good leadership and adequate planning for the venture of another restoration to be successful in the face of a well-organized opposition.

At the accession of George I, indifference on the part of the throne to any attempt at sympathy with the people was only rivalled by the Hanoverians in their lack of understanding of the problems of government. It was opposite in the extreme to the tyranny which the Stuarts had been accustomed to exercise over their ministers, with the result that the latter under the first two Georges acquired a great access of power which had no serious setback until the third generation of the new reigning house. Not until then was a measure of responsibility by the Crown towards the British people recognized and the possession of the English throne regarded as anything but a nuisance and a liability by the new dynasty. Little more than one hundred years before, Charles I had died rather than abrogate the power of government to a hierarchy, even of his own choosing; but by the death of the Martyr the magic spell had been broken. The Civil War had been followed after an interval by the glorious Revolution. Upon the site, the foundations of which were originally prepared by the Long Parliament and further strengthened by those astute ministers who sought the aid of William of Orange, was built the edifice of the great and powerful Whig aristocracy which in the next era was to change England. Never again could the throne regain that autocratic power by which the Stuarts had unsuccessfully endeavoured to hold it.

Later George III more than once was to show himself equal in an emergency to being a power with which his ministers had to reckon; but the old autocracy of the throne was a dead thing. In the environment of political apathy which prevailed under the first two Georges, largely engineered by the crafty Walpole himself, ministerial power continued to wax and flourish amid surroundings of unprecedented subterfuge and corruption. Nevertheless, Sir Robert Walpole, upon whose politics there was, according to the later historians, a mixture of blessings and curses, may perhaps be allowed to be the great man of his time. Whether his qualities were praiseworthy or odious, it is not for us here to pursue. He was responsible for the drastic nature of the change in the land system, but he saw its vital urgency, and we must leave to be justified the means that gained the end, however much his character may have suffered by the gravamen of the charges of corruption levied against him and his ministry. At least he recognized the importance of the food supply and as a corollary raised the value of land by many times. But he turned our energies to the great developments that were opening up at home and would not suffer them to be dissipated in fruitless wars abroad. It must be admitted that his land policy paved the way for a great nation to become still greater, and to enable it within a hundred years to gain the mastery of the world.

The Stuart kings had carefully preserved the rights of the small landed gentry and yeomen. Whether in trueness to the tradition of the Middle Ages, when the throne was their champion against the barons, or out of motives of self-interest, they held the yeomen in great respect, realizing that as a last resort they were the backbone of the country, and could be relied upon to rally in support of the King against any other form of tyranny. With the coming of the new rule and the increasing strength of Parliament the land development of England began to take place at the yeoman's expense. As the power of the throne waned so did their fortunes decline, while those of the great landed gentry, created by the New Aristocracy, came rapidly into the ascendant. Whether by coincidence or design, most members of the Whig party were large landowners and the royal grant became a weapon in their hands for rewarding those who had rendered valuable services to the new régime. For more than a hundred years (1714–1832), beginning with Robert Walpole, landowners virtually ruled England. It was not until the passing of the great Reform Bill, which abolished Pocket Boroughs and Rotten Boroughs, that a large portion of their representation in Parliament was taken away and distributed among the middle classes, the workers in the great industrial cities, and the poorer farming population. The great lords became lords not only of one manor but of many. Hence the manors began to lose their identity and the manorial boundaries their significance under the new system of enclosure that now came into existence.

Before pursuing this theme let us briefly examine the oncoming rush of the Industrial Revolution and some of its implications.

About 1750 it was found that coal and coke could be used in the process of iron-smelting. This great discovery which, more than any other single factor, set in motion the Industrial Revolution, was so far advanced by 1796 that the employment of charcoal for smelting ore had almost ceased except in the most remote areas. The important industry of charcoal burning had been driven across the seas to the Black Forest and to America. Vast iron-works began to be established in the new coal districts in the midlands and the north.

Other innovations ran parallel in point of time with these developments, the most far reaching being those inventions which led to the foundation of the cotton trade and the great textile industry in Lancashire.

The age of iron was attended by the development of communications, and the great works tended to converge on those places where the natural resources of power—coal and water—were to be found conveniently together, and resulted in them concentrating upon entirely new places hitherto of little or no account. Better roads and new water-ways created an improvement in transport which,

in its turn, brought nearer the market needed to consume
this rising output and gave it a breadth undreamed of
before. Soon these products were not only percolating
into every remote place in the country, but there also
remained a considerable surplus available for export
abroad which was more and more eagerly absorbed.

The Black Country with its manifold wares and Lancashire with its textiles throve in their new habitations,
while East Anglia and the pastoral districts in the south
and west correspondingly waned under the gradual lan-
guishing of their village industries. The movement is
another example, common enough in our history, of the
migration of one hitherto flourishing and important sec-
tion of the community to another area as a result of science
and the process of invention. In the England of the
Middle Ages the most densely populated parts were the
southern and eastern counties. In the eighteenth and
nineteenth centuries the position entirely changed with
consequent reactions upon local prosperity.

Sir Charles Petrie[1] says:

'The sparsely populated and agricultural land was becoming
an industrial and urbanised civilisation, and by the time that
George IV was in his grave the link with the older England
had in many cases been snapped. The changes of the early
nineteenth century were so great that by the twenties and
thirties the eighteenth century had to a great extent already
been forgotten.'

Here, then, was the beginning of those economic developments for which the country was ripe. Our purpose
is to trace the effects of this major disturbance upon the
countrymen, the yeomen, and the small-holder and the
landed gentry upon whom they depended, of whom our
friend Twysden, with his property at Roydon, was a
typical example.

Beginning in the midlands and spreading northwards,
the practice of land-enclosure grew rapidly and became
prevalent among the greater landlords, who thereby

[1] *The Four Georges*, p. 224.

sought to conduct farming upon their estates on a larger and better-planned scale. There was a remodelling of farms upon the latest and most scientific lines. The new farmer began to drain his land.

Such men as Joseph Elkington in the latter part of the century were offered inducement by the newly formed Board of Agriculture to give expert advice based upon their own successful experience in those areas where a system of drainage was hitherto non-existent, and to assist in the layout of new enterprises with these modern advantages. Considerable improvement was effected in agricultural machinery and new sowers and reapers were invented. Rotation of crops and scientific cultivation was studied and improved upon. The old system of 'open field' cultivation which had appertained through Tudor and Stuart times was a relic of medieval England and of the very manor itself. In less civilized parts of the country, particularly in the north and in Scotland, it was the only method that could be devised to prevent plundering and to ensure each family that came under the protection of the manor a proper share of the tillage and the produce of the land according to the family status (see chapter on the Manor). The villages and hamlets to which the system was most aptly suited were those which lay scattered in large and desolate tracts of country where relatively few acres were needed to sustain such sparsely inhabited regions. Starting from a centre, the 'open field' expanded outwards into the waste as the little local population grew, each family having its strip of land within the circle. Outside were the common lands, wherein they had their rights of grazing and commonage. Such methods, though adequate for the needs of the time they served, were due for very far-reaching changes in the light of eighteenth-century industrial development and were quite unable to cope with the new needs that followed in its train.

Enclosure meant in effect the annexation of the hitherto free common lands, with compensation, often more apparent than real, for the strips of arable land held by the small tenants. Those who exercised it relied upon the inability of the owners to protect the rights of tenure, of grazing, and of commonage enjoyed by them under the auspices of the Manor from time immemorial. The next step was the proper fencing and division of land according to its farming convenience so that it could be most economically worked on a large scale, to the elimination of extravagance and the space that was wasted in a number of small boundaries. Little wonder that, confronted with a suddenly expanding population in the new industrial centres, these methods were successful; the race between the agricultural and the industrial revolution was hotly pursued on both sides.

That the enclosure system was necessary in the exigencies of the times can hardly be disputed. It was the rapidity of its movement and the ruthlessness of its execution that bore so hardly on our yeomen and poorer countrymen. That it could have been less drastic, less unfairly administered, and more adequately compensated is what could have been wished. The growth of the population in the latter half of the century brought about the necessity of providing much more abundant and cheaper food, a need which the ancient method of farming, with its wasteful and uneconomic system, was incapable of supplying, and which the exacting demands of the Industrial Revolution required that something must be speedily done to remedy.

The opportunity was exploited to the full by the large grain-growing farmer and his powerful landlord, who by this time realized the advantage of letting out his farms on long leases and even investing his own money in co-partnership with his more substantial tenants. While for the most part the enclosure system constituted a new venture in farming, these new areas rapidly outstripped the older prosperous farming counties by reason of the latter being hampered by out-of-date methods and equipment. The new territories had the advantage not only of being laid out upon the most modern lines, but of being adjacent to those industrial centres where the markets for their produce was safely assured.

In East Anglia the growing profitableness of raising sheep was causing their introduction into a country which had hitherto been predominantly arable territory—in fact the granary of England. Sheep-farming, however, required enclosures. The automatic fertility-bearing qualities of the sheep led to the realization of the true value of the animal in the modern agricultural science of that time, and brought about the change in method that was necessary for the proper care and conservation of flocks.

Sheep were folded in winter and fed upon the root crop. Thus the ground was fully manured when the time came for spring ploughing—and the area folded was found to have increased many times in fertility and its consequent yield of grain per acre.

The discovery of the part played by the sheep in the general system of rotation caused a revolution in farming during the seventeenth and eighteenth centuries. Not only were the old deep-rooted ideas upset, but a profound change was brought about in the numerical strength of the population distributed over the chief agricultural centres of England.

The weaving industry naturally tended to settle where the new experiment was being successfully developed, and before long the sheep-farmer was getting a large addition to his income from the value of his wool.

What was the effect of these deep-seated changes upon the hitherto agricultural and self-supporting people of England? They brought about a rapid deterioration in the lot of the peasant-farmer and small-holder, or 'one-field' man, who had always up to this time managed to eke out a fairly happy existence, if not for a large family at least for himself and a modest one. Upon his acre he was accustomed to grow a small crop and to rely upon commonage for grazing his few head of cattle. The ruthless descent upon these common-lands, which were held so easily under the old manors, now began in earnest, and it was not difficult to see that the wielders of political power behind the Enclosures Act were those same new landlords who were invoking legal aid against the *protégés* of the manor, nor was it difficult to understand why the invasions were invariably successful. This was not the only adverse effect upon the peasant. There were a multitude of homely industries practised by a man and his family when not actually engaged at work upon the land.

'The Industrial Revolution', says Professor Trevelyan, 'gradually made an end of two kinds of village industry. It destroyed first the spinning and other by-employments of the wives and children of agricultural families; and secondly the full-time employment of villagers in such various trades as clock-making, basket-weaving, carriage and waggon-building, tanning, milling and brewing, saddling, cobbling, tailoring and the great national industry of cloth-weaving. Some of these arts and industries supplied the village itself, others supplied the national and the world market. In the course of a hundred and seventy years, starting from the accession of George III, British industries have been almost entirely removed to the towns.'

As a result of the Industrial Revolution there ceased to be any local market for the plain home-spun. The rapidity with which prices of handworked goods fell under the weight of machine production led to the gradual disappearance of home-crafts in the cottage, and consequently the abandonment by the village industries of the apprenticeship system which was the time-honoured educational force both mental and physical.

It became clear that there was no further subsidy to be earned by the agricultural labourer to supplement his exiguous wage. The changes in the habits of the people and the disappearance of their local industries affected every dweller of the country-side, not least of all the local squire. The small craftsman was forced to fall back upon such subsistence as agricultural labour could provide, a sum quite inadequate to maintain the average family.

Macaulay[1] tells us that in parts of the country during the short days of winter wages were as low as four shillings a week. The districts of Suffolk and Essex for long remained the best paid, but even there in the summer a man could barely earn a shilling a day, which even allowing for the difference in money values from those to-day, and for the occasionally high price of necessary commodities, was a very meagre wage.

With regard to poor people's dwellings Petrie[2] says:

'Housing conditions had been steadily deteriorating both in town and country. The pulling down of cottages and the refusal to build new ones had resulted in several families crowding into the accommodation previously intended for one. Moreover, young people who, in the days before the enclosures, would have lived in the farms as servants in husbandry or as apprentices, now remained in the cottages with their families.'

Between 1792 and 1801 the Funded Debt had more than doubled as the result of the cost of carrying on war with France. A succession of bad harvests had caused considerable hardship, yet in spite of this the country continued to prosper and the balance of trade remained favourable. Various new methods of financing the heavily increasing debt were resorted to, the most momentous being the invention of Income Tax in 1797 under the prime ministership of William Pitt the Younger. The Bank of England suspended the payment of specie, which was not resumed for twenty-two years.

In the south-east of England the Enclosure Acts brought about comparatively little change in the appearance of the country-side. Enclosure of a less drastic nature had been gradually carried out in Tudor times and had come into existence much about the same time that Roydon was built. In most parts of Kent the fields had already been divided. It was therefore natural that changes which were

---

[1] *History of England*, vol. i, p. 415.
[2] *The Four Georges*, p. 244.

proceeding in the midlands and other rapidly developing parts of England should remain unheeded and even resisted in Kent. Much of the county was unsuitable by the nature of its heavy clay soil and steep downs for large-scale arable farming, for which the flat open spaces of the 'new Counties' were eminently adapted. It has already been observed that these spacious moorlands were mainly open wastes upon which so far no attempt at cultivation had been made.

Roydon gained nothing from the modern methods of agriculture that were being introduced elsewhere. Its chief misfortunes were the fall in the demand for timber and the lack of mature oak which successive owners had found it necessary to cut as times had grown harder. No one since Roger Twysden had lavished the care upon, nor had possessed the expert knowledge of, growing timber that was necessary to maintain its former standard of excellence. Nor had it been possible to make adequate replenishment of the estate since the depredations of the Civil War.

The growing use of iron for shipbuilding and for other commercial purposes, and the decline of charcoal burning in the Kent and Sussex Wealds, which we have already noticed, had their adverse effects on the estate. Roydon timber no longer commanded its former value.

The fortunes of the Twysdens continued to decline. They were not alone in the accentuation of poverty caused by the heavy taxation levied for financing the Napoleonic Wars, which in their turn left a heavy burden of debt for the small land-owner to share.

In 1834 Sir William Jarvis Twysden died and his heir, then aged 46, succeeded to the property. It was so heavily encumbered that he was advised to come to terms of settlement with his mortgagee by disposing of the estate. It was William Cook who held the mortgage on Roydon, and he finally agreed to take over the property in full satisfaction.

In 1837 William Cook decided to make Roydon his

home and soon after this, at the age of 53, he was living there with his wife and family of six children. We will proceed to trace in the next chapter this gentleman's romantic career and see how the son of an obscure Norfolk farmer, owing to the events of the eighteenth century, came to be a prominent and successful merchant in the City of London.

WILLIAM COOK, 1784–1869
by H. W. PICKERSGILL, R.A. (painted *c.* 1827)

CHAPTER XI

WILLIAM COOK OF WYMONDHAM

THE Cooks came from an old Norfolk family of yeomen farmers, who lived near Wymondham. The parish registers of this town show traces of them in the early part of the seventeenth century, when there is recorded the burial of one William Cook. The records vary considerably in the spelling of the name, due partly to the careless spelling of the time and to some extent, perhaps, to an endeavour to differentiate between the various branches of the family. The name appears most commonly spelt Cook or Cooke; only once as Coke (in 1622) and Coak (in 1730), and three times as Coker (between 1733 and 1740).

It is specially recorded in the parish register at Wymondham between 1702 and 1714 that eleven members of the family were 'buried in woolen'. In the days when England was mainly a pastoral country, the production of wool was looked upon as one of the main sources of national wealth, and British wool always enjoyed a wide market, even overseas if there was any surplus available. Its importance grew as the number of sheep-farmers increased with the enclosure system, and consequently a large number of the population became dependent upon the industry. The State commanded the people to wear during five months of the year no garments other than were 'of woolen', and it was declared illegal to be buried in anything but woollen cloth. If the crop was light, it was essential that the home market should secure it at reasonable prices that had not been forced up unduly high owing to foreign demand. On such occasions the export of wool was forbidden by special Act of Parliament. On the other hand, when the crop was a bumper one and there was a glut in the market, this Act was temporarily suspended, and then it was important that every available use of wool should be made in order to maintain the price of a commodity upon which so many depended for their livelihood. Hence the use of it in burials; in 1666 an Act of Parliament was passed decreeing that dead bodies should be wrapped 'in woolen', but owing to frequent evasions a further statute became necessary, forcing people to produce sworn evidence that the law had been complied with. The most natural person to make the affidavit was the parish priest, who, no doubt, made the most of any small opportunity of gain that might proffer itself,whether by a charge for making the entry in the parish register or by granting 'absolution' for a small consideration.

In those days the wool-growers of Norfolk and Suffolk were proverbially prosperous, and the eastern counties were one of the most thickly populated areas of Great Britain. Wool-growing and its subsidiary processes were the mainstay of the country folk of East Anglia, but these industries were fundamentally threatened when Louis XIV, in 1685, revoked the Edict of Nantes and turned on the French Protestants, inflicting upon them the severest persecution and forcing them, even at the point of torture, to go to Mass. At the same time he forbade them to escape the decrees by emigration. Such wide indignation was caused by this intolerance that the religious sympathy of all Protestant countries overcame the fears of a temporary trading advantage, and Huguenots contrived to escape in their hundreds of families to England and the Low Countries. In England they settled at first on the coast of Kent and Sussex, where evidence of them is abundant in the old Cinque Port towns such as Rye and Sandwich. Gradually they made their progress along the seaboard of East Anglia. Their centuries-old trade secrets and successful processes revolutionized the old-fashioned British methods and, although in the long run this was beneficial, for the time being the trade of the remoter regions inland was dislocated, causing much poverty among the smaller farmers. The effects of this immigration began to be felt about the beginning of the eighteenth century and had a

profound reaction upon some of the hitherto most flourishing wool-growing districts, of which north Norfolk,
with Wymondham as its centre, was a typical example.

The Abbey Church of Wymondham was founded in
1107 by William D'Albini, who came over with the Conqueror and was given for his services Wymondham and
other large possessions in Norfolk. He pulled down the
old Saxon church and raised upon its site the Priory of
Wymondham to the glory of the Benedictine Order of
Monks, as an offshoot or cell of the great Abbey of St.
Albans, of which his brother was Abbot. The Norman
church was dedicated to St. Mary the Virgin and was used
by both monks and parishioners, the monks being patrons
of the living. There are still in existence the remains of
their cloisters and domestic buildings, which were very
extensive. At various periods in the Middle Ages the
structure underwent additions exemplifying the contemporary styles of English ecclesiastical architecture
until in 1530, with the inevitableness of the Reformation,
the abbey was dissolved and the monastic buildings de-
molished. Of the latter little remains erect except the
eastern gable of the great chapter house, but the abbey
church was saved for the benefit of the parishioners.
Although the Abbey made Wymondham, there are several
interesting facts to be noted in connexion with the place
itself, for the parish contains 'Stanfield',[1] the home of
Amy Robsart, who first met Dudley on the occasion of
his visit there, when he accompanied his father, the Earl
of Warwick, to quell the rebellion of Robert Kett in
1549. It is the latter event for which Wymondham is best

[1] Stanfield Manor in the Conqueror's time belonged to the Earl de Warren
and in 1256 to Sir Richard Curson. In the sixteenth century it was in the possession of Sir Nicholas Appleyard and was sold by his family in 1563 to Edward
Flowerdew of Hethersett near Norwich. It would appear that during the time
of the Appleyards, the house was let to Sir John Robsart, the father of the
beautiful Amy. Scott in his romantic novel *Kenilworth*, while not pretending to
great historical accuracy in detail, makes no mention of Stanfield, either as the
birth-place or early habitation of Amy Robsart. It is, however, believed—and
Wymondham records lay claim to the fact—that Robert Dudley, later Earl of
Leicester, accompanied his father the Earl of Warwick and stayed at Stanfield
while on their way to meet Kett and subdue the Rebellion.

known in the secular history of England and which, starting in little more than a bitter private feud between two neighbouring squires, bid fair to end with the most serious results.

The grievances which actuated Kett's rising, unlike Wyatt's later rebellion in Kent, which, as we have seen, was for political reasons, were due to the rise in prices, the high rents demanded from the small-holders, and the poor wages paid to the agricultural workers. Above all, the beginning of the enclosure of land, which created such profound unrest in a later century, was the underlying cause. Large landowners were joining together numbers of small farms, turning out the yeomen tenants and substituting hired labour at low wages. They were annexing the waste, or common land, of the manor and depriving the poor of the free keep for their pigs. Many of these changes and the results they had on the local population of the country-side have already been noticed in a previous chapter.

Kett's popularity, in fact, gained him so many followers that he became quite unable to control them, and found himself having to proceed to Norwich at their head, more from the necessity of restraining them from laying waste the whole country-side and burning down the ancient city than from a desire to establish any particular cause. Kett, or Le Catt, whose name signifies 'The Knight', was no labour agitator in modern terms, but a man of considerable property, lord of the manor and zealously affected towards the King, the Church, and the people. We give an account of the rebellion from the late Rev. Martin Jones's book on Wymondham and its abbey.

'His name appears on many papers and documents in the Parish Chest in connection with the old Abbey Church, showing the active interest he took in its welfare, and it was, doubtless, the high-handed methods employed by John Flowerdew, serjeant-at-law, who was appointed by the authorities to superintend the pulling down of the Monastic Building at the Dissolution (every stone of which, as loyal Churchmen, the

Ketts with the other leading families in the town, prized so dear), that was the beginning of the feud which culminated on July 6th, 1549, the Feast of the Translation of St. Thomas à Becket, on which day a yearly fair was held at Wymondham.

'Great numbers of people from the country round came together, as pilgrimages were then made to the shrine of St. Thomas, now known as the Becket's Chapel, around which, doubtless, the people gathered for their Mystery Plays and Games. For it is not so very many years ago that the Becket's Chapel stood in an open plain like the present Market Place.

'This Fair, in 1549, became the occasion of a strong outburst of angry feeling against several Lords of the Manors who had taken advantage of the Act, and had enclosed much of the Common Land in the neighbourhood.

'John Flowerdew, of Hethersett, offered the crowd 40 pence (about 50 shillings in our money), to destroy Kett's hedges in Dykebeck. Kett, who was very popular in the Town, immediately determined on revenge and put himself next morning at the head of a large body of rioters, who went over to Hethersett and cast down all Flowerdew's enclosures.

'The determined and successful way in which Kett carried out their project so pleased the crowd that they immediately chose Robert Kett as their captain, joining with him in command his brother William.

'A camp was formed and a great number of peasants and farm labourers were soon collected on Wymondham Common, which then extended far and wide, including the Meltons, Downham, Browick, Stanfield, &c. Hence the famous Kett's Oak on the main turnpike road between Norwich and Wymondham.

'On July 10th, only four days after the Fair, their numbers had so increased that the rioters broke up from Wymondham and marched on Norwich, crossing the river between Cringleford and Eaton. When about two miles from the city they were met by the High Sheriff of the County, Sir Edmund Windham, who proclaimed them rebels, and commanded them in the King's name to disperse and return to their homes. But his word of warning had no effect and they continued their march. It would appear they passed round the north side of the City levelling all the hedges as they went, crossed the Wensum at Hellesdon, and then through Sprowston they came round to

Mousehold and occupied St. Leonard's Hill, sacking the Palace of Lord Surrey and turning it into a prison. They fixed their head-quarters at St. Michael's Chapel (hence its present name of Kett's Castle), thus they held, from a strategical point of view, a most commanding position.

'Space does not permit, in these brief notes, to give the details of all that happened to the Ketts and their followers in Norwich. How, at one time, they had 20,000 men. How, to feed the same, they raided the country-side near and far. How that, from first to last, Kett did his utmost to keep his motley crowd within bounds. How he fixed a place in the middle of Thorpe Wood where justice might be administered, under a large spreading oak, which received the name of the "Oak of Reformation". How he appointed Thomas Coniers "a certain Minister of the City of St. Martin-at-the-Palace" to say prayers morning and evening in the Camp. How, after many fruitless attempts and much loss of life, they at length managed to get into the City which they held for three weeks against the Royal forces. How they were at length overpowered by Dudley, the Earl of Warwick, on August 23rd, who had been sent down with a large army. How that Robert Kett was hanged on the top of Norwich Castle, whilst William Kett was hanged on the West Tower of Wymondham Church, and how a general Thanksgiving Service was held at St. Peter's, Mancroft, on August 27th, 1549.'

In this quiet old market town William and Mary Cook, in the latter half of the eighteenth century, were raising their children. The family were simple and thrifty folk occupying modest but worthy positions in north Norfolk for many generations. We are not concerned here with their earlier history nor, in fact, until William Cook of Wymondham, who was born in 1756, married Mary Wright in 1779. By that time he was a well-to-do farmer with property in the small parish of Suton, about one and a half miles outside the town, and it was there his family was raised.

The first child Elizabeth died in infancy, but a year later, in 1781, there followed the birth of their eldest son, Edward. We do not hear of him, and must presume that he inherited his father's farm in due course and lived obscurely in Norfolk for the rest of his existence. It is the second son, William, born in 1784, who forms the link in our story. His career is a romance of enterprise and success, and the great merchant-business which he founded in London may well have made his family proud of him. There was another son, Gregory, born in 1786, who later emulated William's example by going to London and making progress with another well-known textile firm.[1] The youngest daughter, Ann, completed the children by his first marriage.

William was only 9 when his mother's death occurred, leaving her husband a widower at 38 with four young children; and so it was that in 1795 he married again and had several more children, one of whom, James, was eventually taken into partnership by his successful half-brother. Another, Elizabeth, later married Groome Howes, the ancestor of another line of partners whom William afterwards took into the firm.

William was very much affected by his mother's death. He had already begun to show that his character was unlike that of any other member of the family and it was his mother who understood him best. It is more than likely that he did not get on well with his brothers and sisters at home, and the death of his mother accentuated these difficulties for him. If she had lived, she could probably have kept him under the family roof, or at least, if he had been destined to go in search of adventure, she could have maintained the ties between him and his home. William evidently did not respond to the call of farming to which he had been born, and took a pessimistic view of such prospects; his portion would have of necessity been a small one and his lot contained little more than the hope of serving under the yoke of his elder brother.

He was away from home a good deal, and frequented the local market town of Wymondham, but there is no evidence that he acquired much in the way of school

---

[1] Messrs. Shoolbreds. In 1820 the firm was Shoolbred, Cook & Co.

education, as we shall see later. During this time he resolved upon the plan of going to seek his living in the Metropolis, where he had heard that there were opportunities for young men who were ready to work hard, of getting into business at a time when merchants were finding difficulty in securing apprentices.

It is necessary to reflect for a moment upon international affairs at the beginning of the nineteenth century and the way they were affecting the state of the agricultural industry in England. Napoleon, after suffering the great naval defeat off Cape Trafalgar, was unable further to challenge Britain's supremacy on the sea. But his armies on land were meeting everywhere with overwhelming success, and Europe was quaking at his victories over Austria and Prussia. The Allies were appalled at the terms of peace which he had forced separately upon the Tsar; none of them was able to withstand his onslaught; and in 1806 a misfortune fell upon Great Britain in the death of her Prime Minister, William Pitt, who had hitherto been the corner-stone upon which rested the whole edifice of European Alliance against the Emperor. At this point Napoleon conceived the idea that if he found it impossible to strike his enemy at the heart he could cut off the supply to the stomach, and that if the supremacy which England had established at sea prevented his successfully invading Britain, he could ruin the trade on which her prosperity depended. He therefore set out to force Europe to boycott England's trade and issued his famous declaration from Berlin that the British Isles henceforth were in a state of blockade; all the European ports of France or her Allies were to refuse to receive ships of the British merchant marine. The 'Continental System' as it was called was a stupendous piece of imagination, and the fact that a similar strategy was employed, and was within an ace of succeeding, in the Great War over a hundred years later, is a tribute to Napoleon's far-seeing genius. It was fortunately not entirely successful, though it did hamper British trade very considerably during the remaining years of the

Napoleonic War, factors which were not without their repercussion upon the country in general and upon the smaller English family inheritances in particular.

These tendencies were not ignored by the astute young William Cook; it appeared to him that the closing of the export markets owing to the war would once again adversely affect Norfolk's wool-growing industry by the fall in the price of wool; consequently the outlook for a farming career, which in any case did not appeal to him, looked unpromising for some time to come.

As a small boy[1] he could remember the hardships caused by the years of bad harvests in the nineties; on the other hand, trade at home was far from inactive and prices of commodities and imported goods were high. The merchanting and industrial sections of the community were prosperous.

In the autumn of 1805, with the heroic news of Trafalgar ringing in his ears, William, at the age of 21, decided on a definite course of action and was determined to go and seek his fortunes in London. We will pass over the admonishments he received upon broaching the proposition to his father and the subsequent leave-taking with his family. Let us imagine his departure, leaving behind, as it turned out for good and all, the quiet uneventful life of the East Anglian farm, heading for the south in the stagecoach, via Bury and Ipswich. The proverbial five golden sovereigns were in his pocket; the frugal amount of baggage containing those small comforts and necessities that his sister had packed for him were his only reminders of home. Arrived at the 'Angel' at Islington with what was left after the depredations of the journey, he proceeded, with many inquiries, to Moorgate and thence to Lombard Street, bound for the Banking House of Overend, Gurney & Co. Approaching the austere portals underneath the sign of the house he searched for a letter—his only introduction to the world of London—procured from his father's attorney in Norfolk, recommending him to the

[1] p. 150.

M

post of clerk in the bank. In those days young men in such a position were fortunate if they got more than five pounds a year and their lodgings, usually over the bank itself. This was certainly not affluence, but it was at least a respectable appointment with prospects dependent mainly on good behaviour and industry, and ensured that the young gentlemen were well looked after, to the great relief and comfort of their parents.

Whether William had any idea of starting on the bottom rung of the ladder and ultimately becoming a banker we have no knowledge. It is probable that the only condition that induced his father to let him go to London was that the young man should take up a respectable position, and possibly Mr. Cook considered that a bank was the only institution in those days that complied with this stipulation. Whatever his intentions were, any hopes he may have had with regard to his prospects at Messrs. Overend & Gurney were speedily doomed to disappointment.

On presenting himself before the partners—no mean ordeal—he was first questioned as to his birth and education, and then sent out to copy a document for his handwriting to be approved. The result was so lamentably bad that with all the good will and recommendations in the world he could not be engaged. The *sine qua non* was a good handwriting and William again found himself outside in Lombard Street. It is possible that he made some use of the interview and that it stood him in good stead, for he was given the address of a client of the bank who was known to be in need of a young apprentice. Determined not to return to the 'Angel' and board the next coach home to Norfolk and humiliation, he wandered disconsolately through the city seeking the address given him. Great Warner Street, Clerkenwell, was very different in appearance to Lombard Street and the fine building which he had first visited. No. 7 was a member of a narrow and dirty street, filled with small merchants making use of the roadway to display their wares amid a noisy turmoil of bargain and barter. William asked for the proprietor and was confronted with Mr. Martin, an elderly but mild-looking gentleman who listened sympathetically to his story, inquired into his antecedents, and finally agreed to engage him, with the usual warning, however, that his appointment would entail hard work, strict punctuality, and good behaviour. Here at least the writing was not of the first importance and William felt confident about his other qualifications.

We will not follow his business career too meticulously. Like Harrison Ainsworth's faithful apprentice to the grocer of Wood Street he gained the confidence of his employer and made steady progress, which is best related in a short account of the firm itself during the early years of its evolution.

In 1809 'Cook & Martin' was well established at the original address in Great Warner Street. William was extremely thrifty and by this time his financial affairs were sufficiently prosperous for him to marry. His wife, Mary Ann Lainson, was a sister of Mr. Robert Lainson, Alderman of the Court of Common Council, of whom he had become a friend in the course of his growing interest in matters connected with the City of London. As a rising young merchant he realized the importance, both for the sake of his own business as well as from a sense of responsibility, of taking an active part in civic life and administration. Soon afterwards he became a member of the Livery of the Worshipful Company of Drapers, aided probably by his brother-in-law's influence.

The war in the Peninsula was now at its height, and Wellington's successes were rallying the cause of the Allies. The blockade was proving less effective, trade was improving, and business had begun to recover.

Mr. Martin was able to retire from active management and William took sole charge of the concern. By 1814 he had saved enough money to buy his old partner out, and in the following year he opened a wholesale establishment at 11 Fish Street Hill, near the Monument. By 1819 'William Cook, Manchester and Scotch Warehouseman' was settled at 89 Cheapside, premises held on a lease from the Mercers' Company. In 1822 he took James, his step-brother, into partnership.

But there came a difficult time during the twenties. The rapid expansion of his business, together with the devastating fall in prices that followed the end of the war—a parallel that closely resembles the times we ourselves experienced one hundred years later—the collapse of trade and agriculture, made it urgently necessary for William either to curtail operations or take in a substantial partner. He followed the latter course, and accordingly took in Mr. John Gladstone, a successful wholesaler with an Irish connexion, and the firm in 1826 became Cook, Gladstone & Co., Manchester, Scotch & Irish Warehousemen. This proved to be a wise move on William's part, and far from suffering any check to its progress the business continued to thrive and expand until it was further propelled by the momentum of trade recovery.

[1]The following extracts from the Minutes of the Court of Assistants and General Court of the Mercers' Company give an interesting account of the negotiations between William Cook and the Senior Livery Company of the City of London for the enlargement and extension of the premises to accommodate his increasing business:

'A Letter dated 28th. July 1825 from William Cook, assignee of the lease of premises No. 89, Cheapside, originally granted to William Hardy, the term of which would expire at Ladyday 1835 was read:

89, Cheapside,
28th. July 1825.

To the Master, Wardens and Court of Assistants of the Mercers' Company.

Gentlemen,

Having agreed with Messrs. Hurst, Robinson & Co. for a lease of the premises, adjoining those in my occupation belonging to your Worshipful Company, for a term of

---

[1] The author is indebted to the Mercers' Company and to Colonel Sir Frank D. Watney, the Clerk, for so kindly making these extracts available.

twenty-one years, and being desirous of communicating with the same, I have taken this opportunity of requesting your permission to do so, and also to solicit an extension of the term of the lease held by me from the Company, making the term twenty-one years, which, should your Worshipful Court entertain, I am willing to surrender that part of the premises under the Hall Kitchen, and to pay for the remainder of the premises, during the term an annual rent of two hundred and seventy-five pounds.

And remain, Gentlemen,

Your most obedient humble servant,

WILLIAM COOK.

'IT WAS RESOLVED—That the offer of Mr. Cook be accepted and that he be permitted to open a communication from that part of the premises to be retained by him, with those adjoining westward, upon condition of his agreeing to close up the same at the expiration of the term.

'At a General Court holden on the 16th. March 1826, the Court authorised the Wardens to affix the Company's seal to the lease of premises No. 89, Cheapside granted to William Cook pursuant to the resolution of the Court of Assistants of the 28th. July 1825.

'At a Court of Assistants, 20th. December 1832, a letter was read from Messrs. Cook & Gladstone, tenants of premises No. 89, Cheapside, requesting to be permitted to make certain alterations to the premises; and that the Company would give them a Lease of the adjoining house No. 88, for a term of twenty-one years at a rent of one hundred and twenty pounds per annum, being the premises at present occupied by Mr. George Hebert at one hundred and eighty pounds per annum, whose term therein will not expire until Lady Day 1835;

'AND IT WAS RESOLVED that Messrs. Cook & Gladstone be informed that the Court are willing to sanction the Transfer to them of the Lease of the house No. 88, Cheapside for the remainder of the unexpired term, and to grant them a new Lease of the same for eleven years from that period at a rent of one hundred and twenty pounds per annum. As also to permit them to make the alterations to the premises, as requested, under the direction of the Company's Surveyor; provided they agree to reinstate the premises in a proper manner previous to the expiration of the term.

'At a Court of Assistants, 31st. January 1833 a letter from Messrs. Cook & Gladstone, tenants of premises No. 89, Cheapside, was read as follows:

To the Worshipful Company of Mercers.

Gentlemen,

We beg to acquaint you that we have made a purchase of large and commodious premises in St. Paul's Church Yard where we intend removing in a few months. We shall not require consequently to make the alterations you so kindly consented to allow us to make in the premises we hold under your Worships; and we beg you to accept our grateful thanks for the same.

Our Mr. Cook intends either to let or sell his premises in Ironmonger Lane which he purchased a few years ago of Messrs. Hurst, Robinson & Co. for nine thousand six hundred pounds and should your Worships be willing to purchase them he will accept of seven thousand five hundred pounds for the freehold of the three Houses.

We remain your Worships' very obedient servants,
COOK & GLADSTONE.

'RESOLVED—That it be referred to the Company's Surveyor to report his opinion as to the value of the premises belonging to Mr. Cook in Ironmonger Lane, offered for sale by him.'

'*Court of Assistants, 24, Decr. 1835.*

'A Member brought under the consideration of the Court the question of purchasing the premises at the south-east corner of Ironmonger Lane, belonging to Mr. William Cook.

'RESOLVED—That it be referred to the Master and Wardens to consult with the Surveyor upon the value of the above property; to consider the expediency of the above purchase and to report thereon to the Court.'

'*Court of Assistants, 17th March 1836.*

'Report of the Master and Wardens upon the value and expediency of the purchase of premises, belonging to Mr. William Cook, at the corner of Ironmonger Lane, Cheapside, adjoining the estate of Henry VIII, was read.

'RESOLVED—That Mr. Smith be authorised, on the part of

the Company, to offer the sum of eight thousand pounds for the purchase of the Freehold of the above mentioned premises.'

'*Court of Assistants, 24th March 1836.*

'The Surveyor's report of his communication with Mr. William Cook respecting the premises at the corner of Ironmonger Lane was read.

Mercers' Hall, 23rd. March 1836.

Gentlemen,

I communicated to Mr. Cook the Resolution of a Court of Assistants held on the 17th. instant relative to the offer of eight thousand pounds for his freehold premises at the Cheapside corner of Ironmonger Lane.

I am requested by him to say he declines that offer but would be willing to make an Exchange with the Company for the premises late in the occupation of Mr. David Evans.

And remain, Gentlemen,

Your faithful and obedient Servant,

GEORGE SMITH.

To the Court of Assistants
of the Mercers' Company.'

'*Court of Assistants, 7th. Octr. 1836.*

'A letter from Mr. William Cook offering to sell to the Company his freehold property at the corner of Ironmonger Lane and Cheapside for the sum of eight thousand five hundred pounds was read.

'RESOLVED—That Mr. Smith, the Surveyor, be authorised to renew the offer of eight thousand pounds for the purchase of the above premises, made by the Company to Mr. Cook in March last; and that this offer be not binding unless accepted within fourteen days from the present date.'

'*Court of Assistants, 14th Octr. 1836.*

'The following report of the Company's Surveyor of Mr. Cook's acceptance of the offer made to him for the purchase of the premises at the corner of Ironmonger Lane, Cheapside, was laid before the Court.

Mercers' Hall, 13th. Oct. 1836.

Gentlemen,

In pursuance of a Resolution of a Court of Assistants held on the 7th. inst. I waited on Mr. W. Cook and offered him the sum of eight thousand pounds for the purchase of his freehold house and premises, corner of Ironmonger Lane and Cheapside in the City of London, which he agrees to accept, but requests the Court will relieve him from the payment of eleven shillings and four pence per annum charged on premises near the Regent's Canal for Land Tax (late the property of Mr. Gregory Wright).

And remain, Gentlemen,
Your faithful & obedient servant,
GEORGE SMITH.

To the Court of Assistants
  of the Mercers' Company.

'ORDERED—That the freehold property of Mr. William Cook,[1] at the corner of Ironmonger Lane, be purchased from the General Funds of the Company. And that Application be made for Licence from the Crown to effect the same.

'RESOLVED—That Mr. Cook be informed the Company are ready to receive any proposition he may have to make for the purchase of the small amount of Land Tax upon premises at Stepney, as mentioned in the Surveyor's report.'

In 1833 William Cook, junior, his eldest son, became a partner and his second son Francis, aged 16, became apprenticed to his elder brother in the same year, whereupon the firm became known as Cook, Son, Gladstone & Co. It is interesting to notice at what an early age the industrialists of that time took in their apprentices and the results this policy achieved. Sir Francis later acquired not only a fortune, but the control of a business upon which hung the commercial welfare of thousands of shopkeepers and traders throughout the Kingdom and the Empire. Having negotiated its property in Cheapside, the firm in 1834 moved to its present situation, 22 St. Paul's Churchyard, and in its modern form is known as Cook, Son & Co. (St. Paul's) Ltd. The company has recently celebrated the 100th anniversary of its trading in St. Paul's Churchyard. Its late chairman, Sir Herbert

[1] The property referred to above, purchased from Mr. Cook, is now known as No. 90 Cheapside, and together with No. 89 is occupied by the Fine Art and General Insurance Company. The whole property was rebuilt in 1880.

Cook, Bt. (a great-grandson of William Cook), retired in 1931, to be succeeded by Mr. Ralph Montagu Cook, the present chairman, another great-grandson of the founder of the original private firm.

After William Cook had acquired Roydon in 1837, he spent much of his time there with his wife and family of three sons and three daughters. The opening of the railway south-east of London to Tonbridge, and its subsequent further extension, enabled him to make the journey to the city often enough to exercise a guiding influence over the business, until his son Francis was thoroughly established and able to carry it on, when the old gentleman saw fit to retire to his country home and enjoy his leisure at Roydon.

In his will he had arranged to leave the property to his much-loved wife for her lifetime, with remainder, at her express wish, to their youngest son Edwin, who was then showing great promise and ability as an officer in the 11th Hussars, with which regiment he fought at Balaclava. Edwin had always shown a great love of the country and especially of horses, and when he came home from the Crimea he found that his father and mother had prepared a fitting welcome for him by completing the new stables at Roydon especially in honour of his return. He won the Grand Military Steeplechase at Warwick in 1845 with 'Torrent', and it is likely that he had in mind the intention of breeding horses near Roydon on pastures similar to those of his neighbour Lord Falmouth, who was building up a famous strain at the Mereworth Castle Stud.

Mrs. Cook died before her husband, and Edwin succeeded his father in 1869; he lived only another three years, barely long enough to see the completion of the very extensive alterations which he and his wife had planned to carry out upon the house, some account of which is given in the next chapter.

Edwin left two sons and two daughters, the eldest son Bertie succeeding after a long minority. He died, unmarried, in 1914 of wounds received in the Great War near Messines after the retreat from Mons, while commanding the First Life Guards and the Composite Regiment of Household Cavalry formed for dismounted action. Roydon and the property passed to his younger brother, Ralph Montagu Cook, the present owner.

THE NORTH FRONT TO-DAY

showing the 19th-century alterations carried out upon the earlier Tudor and Jacobean Front

CHAPTER XII

ARCHITECTURE OF ROYDON: BRICKWORK AND DETAILS

THERE are many difficulties which confront us when we endeavour to trace the original form of Roydon and the subsequent alterations that have taken place since 1535. Owing to these alterations the house has lost a great deal of its character and beauty. The greater part of this loss occurred in the nineteenth century, when much of the original exterior was sacrificed to modernizing the house in the interests of comfort.

The late Mr. Nathaniel Lloyd, when visiting Roydon before the publication of his *History of English Brickwork*, commented regretfully on the disappearance of practically all that was original in the north elevation. He was greatly interested in the brickwork of the garden towers, gateway, and surrounding walls. He compared the garden towers to a pair at Hales Place, Tenterden, some twenty-five miles distant, attributed to the time of Henry VI and was at first of the opinion that they belonged to an earlier date than Roydon itself. Writing generally on these matters he says:

'The gate-way was the immediate successor of the gate-house. In the latter part of the sixteenth century it was no longer necessary to house a guard but only to provide convenient access to the Court or other enclosure attached to the House. The opportunity of emphasising such entrances was seldom overlooked: and although later an entrance might be little more than a door in a wall, the sixteenth century gate-way was second only in importance to the gate-house it superseded.'

The opportunity was certainly not overlooked in the construction of the gateway at Roydon. The imposing arch of projecting layers of purpose-moulded bricks shown in our illustration was flanked with an angular wall of great thickness terminating in octagonal towers at each end, from which the courtyard wall turned back at right angles to meet the house. The work of this wall contains a great deal of characteristic, though not elaborate, brickwork.

The small arched apertures on each side of the gateway were let into niches and built in a style similar to those in the towers themselves. These windows gave a view of the approach to the two watches stationed inside the courtyard, for whom were provided two open recesses each with its brick-seat, fire-place, and chimney-shaft built in the wall, the latter rising to eighteen inches above it. The formal retention of the guard or watchmen was therefore considered still to be necessary at the time when this gateway was built (see chapter on the Manor).

The garden tower shown in our picture[1] is one of two, connected by a wall on a raised terrace running parallel to the house at about thirty yards distance from it. They form a feature of the garden to-day and contain a pretty length of border between two walls, overlooking a bowling-green, now (alas!) the lawn-tennis court.

The towers are within a large rectangle, conforming to the plan of the house and courtyard, and it is probable that there were walls connecting these also, now no longer in existence. Yew hedges have taken their place and produce a pleasant variation in keeping with the original formality.

Much of the evolution of Roydon in its earlier times must be a matter of conjecture, and though we have reliable evidence in the massive rectangular foundation of Kentish Ragstone which enables us to trace the original ground-plan, any attempt at an accurate description of the treatment of the elevation must be largely aided by imagination.

There is considerable variety in the brickwork, both in size and bonding, which tempts us to hazard that there were some different influences at work in the early days, and that considerable intervals elapsed between the various stages of building. A careful examination of the facts gives us some data as to what was done on the house

[1] Frontispiece.

during the first three centuries of its existence. There is no mention in the Diary of Sir Roger Twysden of anything being done to the house, nor is it likely that the disturbed period through which its author lived gave him any opportunity of completing or adding to it. It is recorded, however, that his son, William Twysden (3rd Baronet, 1635–97), 'carried out much work: he repaired and enlarged the Mansion of Roydon, chiefly the east wing'.

This attenuated statement must suffice for supposing that when the said gentleman succeeded on the death of his father in 1672 he set to work to complete Roydon and make it a more imposing mansion. We think there is little doubt that the south front with its large east gable may fairly be attributed to him.

William laid out a large rectangular garden above the terrace, which he enclosed with a high wall. Some of this wall no longer remains, but there is still a gateway at the top which bears his initials and the date W.T. 1683,[1] and if we take this to be the completion of his building enterprise we may conclude that his work on the house took place about 1680. At about this time also he added a porch to the front entrance, in carved stone, decorated in the Renaissance style of the late seventeenth century.[2]

A general survey of the brickwork in and around Roydon indicates what remains of the original structure and what has been added or renewed since 1535.

There are two distinct sizes of brick in evidence, the older (which we shall refer to as the 2 in.), whose dimensions vary in length from 9 to $9\frac{3}{4}$ in., breadth $4\frac{3}{8}$ to $4\frac{3}{4}$ in., and depth 2 to $2\frac{1}{4}$ in., and the more common and later brick which became practically standardized at the end of the seventeenth century, whose measurements are $8\frac{3}{4} \times 4\frac{5}{16} \times 2\frac{1}{2}$ in. In all extensions and repairs the latter has been used throughout, and the earlier restoration work in this size has mellowed so well that without close

---

[1] Upon a plaque over the arch—'W.T. 1683.
                                   'Repaired 1764.
                                   'W.C. 1869'.

[2] Page 140.

examination it cannot be distinguished from the older brick.

There is fortunately plenty of fine 2-in. brickwork left at Roydon. The north porch and the little that remains of the original north front are of 2 in., including the chimney-stacks, as are the towers, walls, and gateway. The garden towers and connecting wall are mainly of 2-in. bricks, with here and there a few courses of $2\frac{1}{2}$ in. where repairs have been necessary. The west side of the house is practically all of 2-in. brick, including the chimney-stacks and buttresses.

It is an interesting fact that the south front is entirely of $2\frac{1}{2}$-in. brick laid in the Flemish bond (alternate stretcher and header in each course), and no attempt has been made to imitate the older bonding in 2-in. brickwork found on the north and west of the house, which is invariably a course of stretchers laid over a course of headers, in what is known as 'Old English Bond'. Wherever repairs were done or new work added, the Flemish bond was, as we have already said, invariably used.

The record of Twysden's work on the house at the end of the seventeenth century, together with the Flemish bonding and the standard-sized brick used, suggest with good reason a much later date of completion for the south front, that is to say, about one hundred and fifty years after the old 'Fortune' was begun.

Mr. Lloyd, very rightly, warns us that an attempt to determine the exact date of any work by the dimensions of the bricks often leads to a wrong conclusion. Generally speaking, bricks of $2\frac{1}{2}$ in. in depth were not in common use until the Restoration, but at Eastbury Manor (1550) the bricks are $2\frac{1}{2}$ in. deep, and again at Stutton (1520) we find a similar brick used, and in a number of other more or less famous Elizabethan houses it is found used in conjunction with bricks of smaller dimension. We must rely, therefore, on bricks of $2\frac{1}{8}$ to $2\frac{3}{8}$ in. in thickness being the general rule, and consider whether the exception applies to Roydon. Nor must the evidence of bonding

SOUTH FRONT, WITH STEPPED EASTERN GABLE

The Bay and Porch were added in the 19th century

be used to draw any downright conclusions. Old English bond continued in general use in this country up to the seventeenth century, when the Flemish bond came into fashion and towards the end of the century began to be generally employed. The latter is used throughout the south front of Roydon; therefore, if we base our conclusions as to the date of this side of the house upon the evidence of the contemporary brick used, we should have to put it at least a hundred years later than the west side. With the knowledge that Twysden carried out considerable work in 1680 we may safely assume this to be a later addition, but we must remember Mr. Lloyd's warning that the evidence of the bonding alone must not be taken as conclusive in determining the matter of the exact date.

It is clear to the observer to-day that the west side retains most of the original features while the north front has had its character obliterated by the alterations of 1869, during which year the east side also was entirely reconstructed. The south front is the interesting one from the controversial point of view.

The elevation is of three stories surmounted by three pointed gables and a fourth of different character, built upon a projection beyond the ground line. It is larger and has been crowstepped to make it a feature distinct from the other three.

It is thought that this gable had at some time been similar to the others and that it was enlarged and stepped at a later period, greatly to the detriment of the appearance of the whole façade.

There are several facts, however, which strongly refute this suggestion and lead us to believe that the whole was designed at the same time and that the east gable, far from being the work of a later vandal, was the purposeful feature chosen by Twysden or his architect for this important aspect of the house. The west side of the house had stepped gables from its inception; it is impossible to say whether the architect of the seventeenth century was required by Twysden merely to complete the south front according to the original plan or to carry it out to his own approved design. At any rate, it would seem to have been fully intended to incorporate something of the character of the west side in the southern aspect. It was therefore designed with three pointed gables, but the character of the house was faithfully represented in the fourth gable, making it the largest and most important feature on that side by projecting it outward and adding steps to adorn it, we venture to think, with admirable effect.

It will soon be seen how vitally important this east gable was to the architect of nearly two centuries later in that it influenced him to employ the crowstepped gable to an exaggerated extent in the transformation of the north front of the house.

It is also an interesting fact that in the building of the stables and laundry during the Crimean War the architect carried out the work in Old English bond, no doubt in the endeavour to be faithful to the character of the brickwork in the west elevation, opposite which they were erected. The aspect when approaching the house from this side is distinctly good, as the house stands well above these buildings and the grouping is effective. It is, moreover, obvious that they were by the same architect as the one commissioned to carry out the alterations on the north front some fifteen years later. He evidently had a strong leaning towards revived Gothic decoration, for he inserted small cruciform windows in the stables, an innovation so far as Roydon was concerned, while on the south side he inserted a tracery window in the newest Gothic style. It is regrettable that these alterations took place at a time when architectural inspiration was at a low ebb in England.

The west side of the house has suffered the minimum amount of alteration and, as we have said, the large majority of the old 2-in. brick remains, laid in English cross-bond—a course of stretchers and a course of headers, stretchers breaking joint, giving a pleasant and informal look.

ROYDON FROM THE WEST

showing the Stables added at the time of the Crimean War

The only alteration that took place was occasioned by the replacement of the old windows by stone-mullioned windows, around which the later 2½-in. bricks were used in the Flemish bond.

The feature of the western side is the survival of the brick mullions in the upper windows under the original stepped gables. These small windows are of purpose-moulded and rubbed brick, which together with the carved brick string-course below them are the best surviving examples of original brick-ornamentation at Roydon.

The chimney-stacks are also fine and the spiral chimneys in front surmounting them are of the best work.

The east side is a contrast to the west. Here the work is recent, for in 1869 the old Jacobean dormers were removed and replaced by wooden dormers of plain and ugly design. A bay was added in the centre of the ground floor, and perhaps the only interesting feature is the large chimney-stack with four finely ornamented spiral chimneys of moulded and rubbed variegated patterns copied from their older brethren.

The chimney-breast is splayed and the flues carried on either side of a set of windows on the ground and first floors. This must have been a 'favourite child' of the architect, and although the effect is not unpleasing, it is somewhat bizarre and quite alien to the character of an Elizabethan house. We have not met it elsewhere in any building of the period. A pinker coloured brick has been used and the bonding, which is Flemish throughout, contains a too frequent use of the blue header at regular intervals which gives the whole work a hard and formal appearance.

Finally we come to the north front, which has borne most of the onslaught of the 1869 alterations, for the architect was unfortunately allowed to give the freest play to his feelings with disastrous results. It is the only side of the house which has been irretrievably ruined, but it is the ancient front and the one which therefore bore the

N

main character of the manor-house from the beginning of its time. Hence our sorrow that the visitor to Roydon is sorely puzzled to-day on seeing a mass of well-mellowed brickwork, and is forced to ask himself whether it really can always have looked like this? On page 55 is reproduced a drawing from a photograph taken some years before the alterations of 1869 occurred, so that we can see exactly what it was once like, and must perforce content ourselves with the past. The east gable (which it will be recalled is crowstepped at the southern end) used to finish to the north with a pretty dormer and lean-to falling towards the front to conform to the slope of the main roof. This extended to the right as far as the large chimney-stack carrying two finely moulded spiral chimneys—the oldest pair on the house. A parapet with three steps extended to the right and joined the stepped gable on the west side. The roof continued above this on the same line, the trough of the large gutter being cunningly hidden by the stack and giving the whole roof the effect of continuing in one unbroken line.

The string-course which we noticed on the west side extended round to the north as far as the angle of the porch, which, with only one room above instead of two as at present, was covered with a pointed lean-to roof. There was a pleasant and informal mixing of Tudor and Jacobean periods in this elevation which could not fail to have been interesting and arresting had it remained as it was before.

The architect of 1869 raised no less than four crowstepped gables upon this elegant front—the large east gable, the centre gable over the porch, one at the west end, and, as if these were not enough, proceeded to cram in yet one more, as though it were an afterthought, between the main chimney-stack and the porch-chimney. Apart from the fussy and overcrowded effect which is the result, he succeeded in completely transforming the house to a point where its character has practically no resemblance to the original, and when, added to this, the

THE EAST END OF THE GALLERY

windows were replaced by the inevitable mullions, the over-effect of the work was complete.

We are not going to deny that the exterior alterations allowed much improvement, by lighting and enlarging it, to the inside of the house. Entrance to the inner courtyard, around which the house was built, was gained by the porch. Windows admitted light from the inner court, but also made the house intensely cold. A large skylight in a massive steel framework was thrown over this inclosure and the internal windows were blocked up in order to give the added measure of warmth and comfort which admittedly were essential.

Up till this time there had been no proper staircase in the house, the only way upstairs having been by a tiny turret stair in use ever since the days of the early manor-house. It emitted from the parlour in the extreme south-east corner. A large oak staircase and landing were now built round the covered courtyard which became known as the hall.

One other thing was done, however, for which we are the poorer, but for which we should have little to quarrel with as regards the internal alterations. That was the cutting away of the western half of the 'long gallery' on the first floor, by far the most beautiful feature of the interior. This was done to form the back landing and back stairs to give access to the domestic offices and the new kitchen. In fairness we must say it could not have been achieved by any other means within the rectangle of the house.

The present generation who live at Roydon have much to be thankful for in these alterations; if they had not been made, the house would, according to modern standards, have been almost impossible to live in. But we cannot help regretting that the architect who carried them out was the same person who perpetrated such unpardonable acts upon the exterior of the house, and that the result was the destruction of so much of the character and beauty of Roydon.

CONCLUSION

WE have seen, within a necessarily small compass, how the tide of events has influenced the land through four centuries, sometimes with a lethargic movement such as one would associate with the country-side, but more often with rapid and profound effect, until the present, with its rate of acceleration and change, has barely been caught up by the past. Yet through this long lapse of time that we have traced its history, Roydon has stood for something that is essentially without change amid all the changes of fortune that have passed over it.

In spite of the transfer of ownership of many country houses, the number and rapidity of which in recent years has been a matter of regret, never was the old French proverb *Plus ça change* . . . more true than of the land and its country estates. Roydon stands not so remotely as once perhaps, but still secure within its own borders. A few carefully guarded acres, a few fortuitously placed trees, ensure for it that immunity from being exploited as a 'site' or from being developed as a building estate with a 'desirable view'.

In all its fifteen generations of owners down to the present day there has been a common factor which, though hard exactly to define, has pervaded each one of them severally, irrespective of their different circumstances and fortunes.

It cannot be claimed that Roydon has more of an atmosphere than scores of other old manor-houses of equal or greater antiquity, but the fact remains that in all of these types of domain, whether great or small, their environment induces a pride of ownership which manifests itself in an hereditary love of them—an intense desire to preserve them intact against all inroads and social onslaughts. The struggle goes on to-day just as it did in the Civil War, but in a different and more insidious form—a gradual pressure exerted by a relentless social advance undermining the strength and foundations upon which these inheritances were originally built and the conditions under which they were once able to thrive.

How long can they continue to survive it? While the stability of the country-side hangs in the balance, it seems that the pendulum is swinging back in favour of a more lenient attitude towards the country and all that it means in the life and economy of the nation. Recent signs point to this fact being recognized at last, lest some of the soundest traditions upon which our national life has been founded should finally perish. The scheme being considered by the National Trust to take over ownership of certain historic properties on similar lines to the French Association, which has made much progress in the acquisition of 'La Demeure Historique', is likely to meet with an interesting career and to be discussed widely and sympathetically. Nevertheless, it is likely to be availed of only as a life-line when everything else has been jettisoned, and when many families have already long since been forced to sever their connexion with their ancient home, if not actually to dispose of it. It would seem that a more humane operation could be evolved that would not entail the parting with actual ownership; breaking perhaps the continuity of many generations of proud and loving possession by owners, who not only lavished their wealth and care upon their own estates, but because of their position, instinctively performed countless unobtrusive acts of kindness in their own small fragment of England.

Those who still strive to keep up the manor to-day cannot be blamed if, in a modern social system that takes justifiable pride in having become self-supporting, they take a different view of their duties and responsibilities to that of their ancestors.

Several factors will have a dominating influence in the near future for good or bad, according to how the issue turns out. Rigid control of building plans by sets of authorities over wide areas and the prevention of a tendency for buildings to straggle are the most urgent and crying needs of the moment. The improvement of the town areas, to redress their relative unattractiveness *vis-à-vis* the country as a medium in which to live, is another essential adjustment to be made. Still more requisite for our national and social economy is the raising of the status of the agricultural worker to a level more in accord with his brother in the factory or town, coupled with a system of education and training in the vocation of the land.

Finally, the burden weighing upon the landed proprietor must be lightened, especially death duties on agricultural property. For some reason or other he is invariably singled out by the social reformer as the villain of the piece, possessing unearned, and therefore invidious, wealth. The land for the people—the project of nationalizing the land—has long been hankered after and will always be proved an illusion so long as an ever-rising standard of living is looked for, and human beings seek to achieve a higher attainment of desire. Nor is it conceivable that the English race will voluntarily sacrifice, or even for a moment jeopardize, its liberty; but it is abundantly clear that state ownership of land, demanding as it does intense nationalistic policy to support it, spells the end of freedom.

Throughout all time there have been good landlords and bad, as also there have been tenants and labourers industrious and idle. They may be safely left to find their own level by the same economic processes that have served so well and that will inevitably discover it. The landowner of the future can no longer be an idle partner in the land. Either he must be his own steward and see to it that every part of his land is productive, or he must contribute from some outside business source the steady flow of money essential to the upkeep of his estate. To satisfy the constant need of the land, capital must be encouraged to flow into it, not driven out. Estate duty, payable at the critical time of succession, more often than not leads directly under present circumstances to the disintegration of the estate itself, an effect which surely cannot be intended and must be most prejudicial to farming. The tenant, who seldom has more than the bare minimum of capital upon which to run his business as a going concern, cannot be expected to provide means to keep the fixed assets of the farm in a proper and efficient state of repair. Therefore some easement of this burden should be made before more damage is done and to such amendments of policy should government be alive, if it is to play the role of a benevolent and thoughtful parent directing the latent energy of a neglected and disgruntled child.

The reader who has patiently borne with these chapters illustrating various phases of country life over a long period may bear with us if this book ends as it began—with a plea that our best forces be mobilized in defence of our oldest and most priceless heritage. To secure this requires a measure of foresight based upon a clear understanding of modern political and social trends, coupled with a new teaching that brings home to our people the conviction that they neglect the good earth and its amenities at their peril.

INDEX

Abell, H. F., 80, 82.
Abolition Bill, 137 *n*.
Addiscombe, 44.
Agriculture, Board of, 146.
Ainsworth, Harrison, 68, 163.
Alexandria, 26–7.
Allington Castle, 6, 53, 65–6, 69, 74–6.
America, 144.
'Angel, the', Islington, 161–2.
Anglia, East, 145, 148, 154.
Anne, Queen, 61, 141.
Anne, Queen of Denmark, 76.
Appleyard, Sir Nicholas, 155 *n*.
Architecture, 6–7, 20–5, 52–9, 84, 140, 171–9.
Aristocracy, the New, 143.
Armada, the, 65.
Ash, John, 131, 135.
Ashford, 17, 61.
Astley, John, 75.
Austin, Mr., 135.
Aylesford, 45, 68, 129, 140.
  Earl of, 129 *n*.
  Light Horse, 65.

Baker, Sir John, 15.
Banbury, 134.
Bank of England, 150.
Barming, East, 45.
Battle, Great Abbey of, 63–64 *n*.
Beauvais, Martin de, 20.
Becket, St. Thomas à, 22, 157.
Beckhal, 37, 40.
Bedingfield family, 37–40.
Belchamp St. Paul, 71.
Benedictine Order of Monks, 155.
Bennitt, Rev. F. W., viii, 32.
Bigge, Edward, 47.
Birling, 41, 43, 45.
'Bishops, Utter Abolition of', 29.
Black Canons, Cloister of, at Oxford, 10.
  at Tunbridge, 33 *n*.
Black Country, the, 145.
Black Death, the, 23.

Black Forest, the, 144.
Blackheath, 17, 83, 97, 99.
Blacksole Field, 69.
Black Prince, Edward, the, 13 *n*.
Blankney, 74.
Blount, Mr., 97.
Bodiam, 6, 53.
Boleyn, Anne, 74.
Boroughs, 'Pocket' and 'Rotten', 144.
Boughton-Malherbe, 17.
Boxley, 45.
Bradbourne, viii, 60, 85, 104 *n*.
Brand Bridges, 43 *n*.
Brenchley, Parish of, 28.
Bret, Captain, 68.
Bridge Croft, 13–14.
Bristol, 114, 124.
Brokar, Ralph, 24.
Bromes (Lomewood), 10, 42, 45.
Bromley, 110.
  Sir John, 33.
Brook, Sir Basil, 103.
Brooke, Walter, 129.
Browick, 157.
Browne, Richard, 134.
  Sam, 127–8.
Buckingham, Duke of, 17.
Bunckly, Sir George, 90.
Burgavenny, George, Lord, 41–2, 69.
Burnham, 45.
Bury, 161.
Butler, Sir William, 104.
Byron, Lord, 141.

Cabal Ministry, 84.
Cade, Jack, Rebellion of, 16–18, 33.
Caerphilly, 6.
Cambridge, 77.
Canterbury, 10–14, 19, 20–3, 31, 42, 64 *n*., 75, 107–8.
  Archbishops of, 10–12, 33 *n*., 64 *n*.
  Cathedral, 20.
  Saxon Cathedral, 12, 22.